# our money ourselves

Except for the women who have given permission to be identified, the names and identifying characteristics of the other women in this book have been changed in the interest of confidentiality.

The publisher and the authors do not assume, and hereby disclaim, any liability to any party for any loss or damage caused by errors or omissions in *Our Money, Ourselves: Redesigning Your Relationship With Money*. This book is designed to be a guide, not a replacement for professional counsel, whether therapeutic or financial. It is sold with the understanding that the publisher and the authors are not engaged in rendering therapeutic or financial advice.

a self-help guide

# our money ourselves

## REDESIGNING YOUR RELATIONSHIP WITH MONEY

## Dr. C Diane Ealy and Dr. Kay Lesh

AMACOM
American Management Association
New York • Atlanta • Boston • Chicago • Kansas City • San Francisco • Washington, D.C.
Brussels • Mexico City • Tokyo • Toronto

Library of Congress Cataloging-in-Publication Data

Ealy, C Diane.
    Our money, ourselves : redesigning your relationship with money /
C Diane Ealy and Kay Lesh.
        p.   cm.
    Includes bibliographical references (p.   ).
    ISBN 0-8144-7999-5
        1. Women—Finance, Personal—Psychological aspects—Case studies.
    2. Money—Psychological aspects—Case studies.   I. Lesh, Kay.
    II. Title.
    HG179.E226   1998
    332.024'042—dc21                                            98–25714
                                                                    CIP

Printing number

10   9   8   7   6   5   4   3   2   1

# Contents

# *A*cknowledgments

Every book happens with the support of numerous people. First, we thank the many women who have taken part in our workshops and participated in our questionnaire, giving us insights and delicious quotes that have helped us understand women's relationship with money. Our agent, Elizabeth Frost Knappman, was unwavering in her support for this project. Every author should have the enthusiastic support we have had from Ellen Kadin, Irene Majuk, and the rest of the staff at AMACOM. Liz MacDonell's insights, as always, helped improve our ability to communicate. Finally, we are grateful for the love and continuous support of our immediate and extended families, including the cats and dogs.

# $\mathscr{P}$reface

We invite you to not just read this book, but to participate in it. For too long, women have usually groaned at the suggestion that they do something with money. A friend once asked us, "If I go to your money workshop, will I have to balance my checkbook?" "Not unless you want to," Diane replied. Besides, our workshops are about relating to money in healthy ways, not about the mechanics of handling financial affairs.

Finding out information about good investments, developing a budget, negotiating for better salary, or any other money management issue is easy. And you can acquire that information from sources that suit you—seminars and workshops, books, television programs, magazine articles. So why do women often neglect to put into practice the knowledge they have about handling money? This question motivated us to develop workshops and to write this book.

Although we still have a way to go to attain equity, women have made great strides in the marketplace. Our salaries are rising. As a group, we are better educated, hold more responsible positions, and, generally, have more career possibilities than our mothers. Yet one area remains where women have made minimal progress—how we relate to money. We are progressing in virtually all other areas of our lives. Money issues are a kind of last frontier in our development.

Like any other attempt to move forward in our personal growth, dealing with beliefs about money and the effects those beliefs have on our current state of being can be both a treacherous and an exciting journey. While the subject of money is certainly very serious for most of us, how we go about redesigning our relationship to it can be fascinating, even fun. And we want to encourage you and guide you on your way.

In the first three parts of this book, we ask you to look at the ideas you currently hold about money and to examine where these came from. In addition, we offer exercises to help you shed those concepts that are unhealthy for you. Negative beliefs drive negative behaviors. We can have all kinds of information about investing, but avoid doing so because of some deeply held beliefs. It's time to get rid of these messages.

Then, in Part Four, we offer you a new way to view money. Currently, most of us live with a belief system that was designed by those few who want to have power over the many. We have strong cultural beliefs that help keep most people in a depowered and unbalanced position regarding money. We believe the time has come for women to redefine money according to how we want it to serve us. Developing new concepts about money is a significant part of women stepping fully into our own power.

We suggest here some very different ways to relate to money, ways that may at first seem odd. We ask only that you consider some alternative, positive relationship to money. We hope that out of your experience with this book will come a more powerful you who experiences money as just another tool to help you improve your life and to have more fun! We envision women from all backgrounds and socioeconomic levels joining in a healthy redesigning of the place they want money to hold in their lives. We see women taking charge of their financial circumstances in empowering ways, using the information available to them to improve both their own lives and the lives of their children. You are a part of this vision.

# The Maiden and the Marketplace
# (A Money Fable)

In a long ago time and far away land lived a young maiden. This maiden wanted to be a good girl. She wanted even more to grow up to be a virtuous woman. So she listened carefully to the teachings of those who were older and wiser than she. Sometimes she would hear her mother or her grandmother telling her different things than they told her brother. But she decided that was all right, because they wouldn't teach her the wrong things. She tried hard to follow this path of wisdom as she grew up in a world that was often confusing.

One day Grandmother gave the young maiden ten coins and asked her to journey to the marketplace in town to get food for their larder. The maiden was pretty sure that she needed more than ten coins to restock their larder, but remembering the teachings of her elders, she knew she shouldn't ask for more. "I don't like talking about money and just couldn't ask for more. It'll be all right," she thought. "Besides, I probably don't deserve more anyway."

As she walked along the path to town, the maiden passed a number of beggars. Some even held up signs that carried sad messages like "will work for food" or "homeless vet, can't feed family." Again messages about money and putting others first flashed through her mind, so she gave all who asked part of her supply of coins. "This is what a virtuous woman would do," she reassured herself. By the time she reached the marketplace, she had only two coins left.

Because she was weary from her journey, the young maiden sat in the shade of a tree to gather her energy before entering the marketplace. While she rested, a charming young lad stopped by and, after chatting awhile, graciously offered to do her shopping for her. "Nobody takes maidens seriously in the marketplace. I can do it faster and besides, I know people who will give me special rates. Why, I can get you ten coins' worth for your remaining two," he bragged. This sounded good to the maiden. She was a little frightened of the marketplace anyway and wasn't sure she knew how to get the most for her money. She gave the lad her remaining two coins and, feeling relieved, sat back to enjoy the cool shade.

The young maiden waited patiently for a long time. Finally, after she could wait no longer, she decided to see what had happened to the lad. Bravely she entered the marketplace. She questioned several shopkeepers about the lad and discovered that he had not been to their stores. Eventually, the maiden realized that he had never intended to help her and instead had run off with her remaining coins.

The young maiden sat by the entrance to the marketplace crying bitterly. She was very confused—she had done what she thought a good maiden should do, but now she had neither money nor goods and feared going home and admitting her mistakes. As she sat there in her helplessness, two old women stopped by to inquire the cause of her tears. When they heard the maiden's story, the first old woman laughed and said, "Silly girl. You are young and pretty. Why don't you just sit here and wait? The Prince will be coming this way soon. I'm sure he'll rescue you. He does that a lot these days. I hear he enjoys it."

The second old woman said, "In my opinion, young girls don't belong in the marketplace anyway. It's just not virtuous. Wait for a Good Provider. That's the solution!"

The young maiden was happy to hear these wise words. They

sounded like the lessons she had been learning at home. She had heard about Princes and Good Providers, and they sounded much less scary than facing the marketplace alone. Confused no more, she now knew exactly what she needed to do. With a renewed sense of purpose, the maiden arranged her clothing so that it would be most flattering to her figure, fixed her makeup and hair, and sat down to wait.

At last report, she was still waiting.

# Part One
## Early Lessons

*Chapter One*

# Getting Started

Several years ago, we began conducting workshops for women to help them look at their money issues. Our reception was mixed at best. Women told us that this was a great idea for a workshop and was much needed. "Boy, I could really benefit from something like that," was the most common feedback we heard. Then, when the day of the workshop arrived, attendance was sparse. We realized that women were uncomfortable examining their emotional ties to money. They wanted to dismiss the possibility that their relationship with money was unhealthy or failed to serve their best interests. And they wanted to avoid any possibility of having to discuss specifics about money, such as how much they earned, with others.

Today, things are somewhat different. While it is true that more women are seeking information about ways to increase their financial security, that knowledge will be worthless as long as their total relationship to money remains unexamined. Studies are showing us that because some women avoid developing a healthier rapport with money, they are losing income. These women are often poorly prepared for retirement or are missing out on increased income at work or from investments.

Our goal in writing this book is to help women look at the financially inhibiting money messages they receive. Our intention is to shine a light on the concepts that hold women back and to design new, healthier, more enjoyable ways to relate to money. The time has come for women to clear the way for developing a more powerful connection to money, even to redefine what money means. We have all accepted society's definition of money, including its purpose and function in our lives. Now we are going to take you on a journey to help you reconceptualize money and redefine its function. We propose that seeing money as a form of energy and that understanding money's spiritual aspect will enable you to develop a healthy relationship with money.

We believe many women have received messages in their lives telling them they are somehow inadequate to handle money—just because they're women. Or that being competent with money is unladylike. Or that women don't have to worry their "pretty little selves" about it because someone else will take care of it for them. It's time to get rid of these messages and develop a belief system about money that you want to live with.

Throughout this book you will encounter a number of exercises designed to help you look at the messages you have received that form your particular relationship to money, resolve the less than positive issues, and create a healthy, new relationship with money. Then we will reconceptualize and redefine money on our terms. We hope that as a result of using this book you will gain a more solid sense of your financial future, which, in turn, will enable you to be freer and more independent. We invite you to participate in this book with a spirit of adventure and curiosity. We're going to ask you to discard beliefs about money that keep you from living the kind of life you want. And we encourage you to explore new, more powerful ways of relating to and defining the meaning of money. We hope you will have fun with this experience.

## Exploring Your Money Attitudes

In this society, talking about money is tricky business. Nothing is so secret, so personal, as how much money we make, what our homes cost, or the amount we have in the bank and in investments. In an age when we are encouraged to tell all in group therapy, personal growth workshops, and twelve-step programs, "all" certainly does not include money. We have witnessed people telling us, along with a group of strangers, about extremely personal experiences—spousal abuse, physical, emotional, and sexual abuse as children, violent fits of temper, sexual excesses. People are willing, some are even eager, to disclose all sorts of sordid and lurid personal events. But we have learned not to ask about money. That's too personal! Besides, it's not anybody's business, is it?

One thing is for certain—if you want to avoid dealing with an issue, if you want the status quo to be maintained, don't talk about it. Keeping a veil of secrecy around money only serves to continue to build a mystique about it.

We find that women are often reluctant to talk about money even to themselves! Think about your own attitude when it comes to your paycheck or to paying bills and managing a budget. Can you look at these things objectively or are they fraught with emotion, denial, or even avoidance? As therapists, we have noted how often people who have shared their innermost secrets hesitate in talking about their income. We have observed the same phenomenon as workshop leaders.

How often do you discuss—not argue about, but truly discuss—money and how you relate to it with your partner? Do you each assume you know the other's feelings and attitudes? What we can observe regarding a person's behavior relating to money isn't always a true indicator of what is going on beneath the surface. How do you react when we even suggest such a conversation? Do you get a sinking or queasy feeling in the pit of your stomach? Many of our workshop participants have reported having this sort of reaction. Taboos around talking about money run deep through our society. To maximize your benefit from going through this book, you will have to overcome this prohibition, at least in private, when looking at your issues.

This society teaches us that money is very much a part of our worth as individuals and is integral to how we should define ourselves. A major goal of this book is to put these two fallacies to rest. But these beliefs inspire a myriad of unhealthy behaviors concerning money:

- If I tell someone else how much or how little money I earn, then my worth as a person will go up or down accordingly.
- I judge my own worth, or lack of, according to my income.
- If we are friends, and you start earning significantly more than I do, we may no longer be able to remain friends.
- If we are partners, and you start earning significantly more than I do, we may no longer be able to remain together.

This connection between money and personal worth is definitely something we learn in this culture. Diane remembers a conversation with a colleague who had spent several years working for businesses in Taiwan. She was a liaison between Chinese companies and the Americans who came to conduct business. She explained her major challenge:

> Every time some Americans would come into town, I would have to coach the greeters on what they would talk about on the ride from the airport to the hotel. Inevitably, when I would ask them what they intended to discuss, they would reply that they planned to ask the visitors how much money their company makes as well as how much money they each earn. I would explain that this was not proper conversation, that instead they should ask about their families, about how their flight was, things like that. And I knew what the reaction would be to my suggestions—shock. ''I can't talk about those things,'' they would say. ''That's too personal.'' Quite a different standard.

significantly more or less money than you do? Try this sentence completion:

When I talk about how much money I make, I _____
_____.

Talking about how much money I make or anyone else makes
is _____
_____.

When the subject of money comes up, I _____
and I feel _____.

We want to encourage you to become more comfortable than most people are in talking about money. In gathering information for this book, we circulated a questionnaire that we have duplicated at the end of this chapter. At the bottom, we asked people to state how much money they made. We believed that we needed this information to determine if income level seemed to influence a set of beliefs, or if certain experiences or beliefs were common to particular income levels. We found no such patterns. At the same time, we wondered how many women neglected to return the questionnaire because they didn't want us to know how much money they earned. We have no way of knowing the answer to that. But we do know that the subject is a sensitive one in this culture and we hope that you will put aside any sensitivity you may have about discussing your money issues, at least with yourself.

As you accompany us on this journey to a healthier relationship with money, we want you to be as open with yourself as you can. And we will continually suggest that the money messages we have gotten from this society need to be closely examined and, frequently, need to be replaced with healthy beliefs. So let's relax our attitudes about money discussions and begin our journey.

## As We Begin

Even though we have worked in this area for many years, when we decided to write this book, we also decided that we wanted to have women's direct input into the issues we were exploring. Hence, the questionnaire.

We hoped that the women who participated would respond to every question, so we made the questionnaire short. Much to our surprise, not only did most women complete the questionnaire, but they also wrote on the backs of the pages and even added pages. Many women told us that answering the questionnaire was a powerful experience for them. They said they wanted to complete it for themselves, to learn more about their money messages. And they told us it brought out aspects of themselves that they were currently grappling with.

So, before you go any further with this book, we invite you to participate in our questionnaire, too. Read through the questionnaire first, taking a few minutes to reflect on money and what it means to you, then answer the questions from your heart. Keep in mind as you respond that we will deal with the topics brought out in the questions throughout the book. So take your time with your answers. We will also share other women's reactions with you. Not only are their responses interesting, but we also think you will discover that you are not alone in your experiences and how they have shaped you. We urge you to let curiosity be your companion as you explore these questions.

● ● ●

1. What messages did you get as a child about money and earning money?

2. How have these messages influenced you as an adult?

3. Please complete the following sentences in three different ways: first, as you think your mother would; second, as you think your father would; third, as you would. (If you were raised by someone other than your mother and/or father, note whom you are responding for.)

(mother) Money is _____.

(father) Money is _____.

(self) Money is _____.

(mother) When I think about my relationship with money, I recognize that _____

_____.

(father) When I think about my relationship with money, I recognize that _____

_____.

(self) When I think about my relationship with money, I recognize that _____

_____.

(mother) Security is _____.

(father) Security is _____.

(self) Security is _____.

4. What role, if any, does money play in your sense of security?




5. What is your worst fear concerning your self and your financial security?




6. Please comment on the following areas as they relate to you.

   Money and self-esteem:

Asking for what you're worth:

Money as energy:

Money and relationships:

Spiritual nature of money:

Your ideal relationship with money:

7. Jot down any additional thoughts you may have about money.

*Chapter Two*

# &xploring Your Money Messages

Do you remember when you were a child and you got "the look" from a parent? You know, the look that told you your behavior wasn't appropriate. You understood exactly how that parent felt about you—no words needed. The impatient sigh, the frown, the eyes rolled upward told us without words what we needed to know about life in our family. A woman in one of our workshops described an expression her mother used that combined hurt and disappointment in a powerful yet silent way. "I knew exactly how Mom felt, even though she never said a thing." In a similar way, little boys, ignored for crying when hurt, quickly learned that tears were not acceptable behavior according to the adults around them. Little girls, rewarded for quiet play with their dolls, came to understand what was expected of them. These *indirect messages* were implied rather than spoken, felt rather than heard.

In the process called *socialization,* we learned from our family and other important people what we should and shouldn't do. Some instructions came in the form of indirect messages while others were delivered as *direct messages*. For example, we were taught that it was important to mind our parents, show respect for our teachers, and look both ways before crossing the street. These direct messages helped us know what to do and how to behave. Both types of messages, the indirect and the direct, had power. They shaped our world for us, told us what to do, what to believe, and even how to feel.

Knowledge about how to deal with money arrived in much the same manner. We absorbed both the direct and indirect messages regarding what we should and should not do. As we watched and listened to the adults in our lives, we figured out how to act, think, and feel about money. Our money messages, like all the other messages from our families and society, had a powerful effect on our current attitudes and behaviors. Thus, changing our personal money story means we need to know what messages we carry with us and to understand their development and how they affect our present-day behaviors.

Like the maiden in the fable, the messages you receive about money are both *direct* and *indirect*; that is, they are both conscious and unconscious. Only by looking at both types of messages will you get a complete picture of your "money self." Armed with this information, you can then be empowered to change any harmful perceptions and deal with money issues in a straightforward, productive manner. You can even define money on your own terms.

Let's look at the money messages you may carry. We start with direct messages, which are in some ways the easiest to tap into because they are conscious. However, whether they are conscious or unconscious, be aware that most of your money messages are loaded with strong emotion. It's unlikely that your personal beliefs include all the messages we talk about. What's important is that you recognize the ones that do apply to you.

## Direct Messages

Direct messages are the easiest to identify because they are the ones you grew up hearing from significant adults and in the media. These are the messages that can be easily brought to mind, the stereotypes that define what men and women are "supposed" to do regarding money. Common messages include the notion that if a woman is a "good girl," then a knight in shining armor will come to rescue her from her money concerns. Meanwhile, men are given the message that they have to be that knight. Even at a young age, boys are treated as if they know how to handle money. Society simply expects it of them, whether they know about money or not.[1]

As a result, men tend to act confident about money matters even when they are secretly frightened. Women, on the other hand, play the role of the distressed maiden—they behave in fearful ways around money and money decisions, even to the point of becoming easily panicked.[2] Consider how these messages manifest themselves: When men make money in the stock market, they take credit for their expert decisions; when they lose, they blame others. When women make money in the stock market, they generally give credit to external influences such as luck or good advice from a broker; however, when they lose money, women blame themselves.[3]

You may also have heard direct messages around issues such as whether it's appropriate for married women to work outside the home. If a woman is forced by economic circumstances to do so, as most women now are, her work tends to be looked upon as supplemental income for the family, not as a rewarding, stimulating career. Granted, this can be cause for resentment by the man who is supposed to be the primary breadwinner. He may be jealous of his wife's situation, seeing her as having the option to generate income or not.[4]

In our workshops, one way we help participants get in touch with direct messages is by asking questions about their money memories. For example, Wanda, a homemaker, told us how her older and younger brothers were allowed to have a variety of part-time jobs, while she was restricted to doing baby-sitting for neighborhood children, even when she was old enough to do other types of work.

Dad and Mom said that they didn't want me working in places where I might be exposed to what they called ''rough characters.'' I always envied my brothers because it seemed that they got to do more interesting jobs than I did. Of course they made more money, too. You sure don't get rich baby-sitting! Looking back, I can see that the rules had more to do with their messages about suitable work for women than about reality.

Wanda's explicit messages were clear: Men make more money, have more interesting work, and are safer in the workforce than women.

Our society reinforces these gender differences in the media. Study after study of prime-time television programming shows women as dependent on men and mainly concerned with home and relationships. (These same women, we might add, are significantly thinner and younger than the average female viewer is.[5]) Even Murphy Brown, the tough, aggressive newscaster played by Candace Bergen, had to be softened by having a baby. Few TV shows portray women as career focused or concerned with earning power—most are still focused on their looks or relationships.

The media also mirrors society's mixed feelings about women who have money. They are frequently seen as incomplete women. Glenn Close as the evil seductress in the film *Fatal Attraction* is successful but psychotic. Demi Moore in *Disclosure* has achieved success in the business world but is unbalanced and spiteful. In real life, Leona Helmsley garners much more enmity in the press than Charles Keating does for similar activities. When we ask workshop participants to think of derogatory names or stereotypes that are applied to women with money, the words flow. Such terms as "rich bitch," "gold digger," and "fortune hunter" emerge, as do stereotypes like: "She slept her way to the top," "She is only working for pin money," or "Sure, her management team gets results, but she's a cold fish." This lack of a balanced perspective reinforces a message that money is not a suitable concern for a truly feminine woman. This either/or view contributes to our inability to place money in its proper perspective—as a tool to help us toward independence, not an end in itself.

Another powerful message revolves around family loyalty. In some families, accepting the family beliefs and behaviors shows loyalty. Your views of what men and women do with money can become a loyalty issue. Going against the family views can be a painful test of independence. And rejecting a family message usually only happens with a struggle. The exercise at the end of this chapter will help you gain a clearer picture of your family dynamic.

In the meantime, to understand some of your direct family messages, complete the following exercise. We encourage you to write out your responses so you can refer to them later.

1. What did your mother believe about her family role regarding money?

2. What did your father believe about his family role regarding money?

3. Who made the financial decisions in your family? How were decisions reached? Was one parent a tightwad while the other was a spendthrift? Was there conflict over roles?

4. If your parents fought about money, was there a particular recurring issue? What role did you take? Were you on either parent's side? How about your siblings, did they take sides with either parent?

5. What messages did you receive from religious teachings regarding the place of money in your life?

6. What was the predominant view of money in your school and neighborhood?

7. Are you aware of any cultural or ethnic messages about money? Did you hear any stereotypes?

8. Regarding your role with money, complete the following sentences:

My father would be proud of me if I _____
_____.

My mother would be proud of me if I _____
_____.

9. What were your parents' views about the work/money connection? Was work fulfilling? A necessary evil?

10. Are there other messages you can list?

The answers to these questions will help you identify and clarify some of the explicit family messages you carry with you as an adult. As you capture your past messages, you will begin to see how they help define your thoughts and actions today. While we explore the subject of workplace money messages later, start thinking now about how your family messages may be playing themselves out at work. Does the organization you work for hold views about money that are similar to the ones you learned in your family?

Other beliefs may pop up as you continue through this book as well—you should write them down as they appear. When you become aware of your direct messages, you can rewrite them in a more positive way. The following exercise demonstrates one way to change a direct message.

One of your beliefs may be that as a woman you make poor money decisions. To help you redesign this message, think about a decision you have made that worked out well, that brought you rewards. It doesn't matter if it was money related or not; the point is to recall the decision and the positive feelings that went with it. Or, seek out women in your community whom you see as successful. Talk to them about their sense of self-worth, their relationship to money, and their decision-making process. People love to talk about themselves and most are very willing to share their stories of success. Strong mentor relationships can grow out of these discussions.

Next, design a powerful, positive statement that you can make to counteract this destructive belief. The idea with this approach is to replace the negative message with one that will enable you to move into a more positive relationship with money. To counter the notion that you make inadequate money decisions, begin writing out a statement that you would like to be true, for instance, ``I make sound money decisions'' or ``I am confident in my money decisions.'' Make certain the statement is in the present tense and contains simple, concise, precise, positive language.

Now, as was first suggested, recall an instance when you made a rewarding decision, regardless of whether or not it had to do with money. And don't be concerned about whether or not it was a ``big'' decision. Any size will do. Relive that decision, paying special attention to the feelings that went along with it.

Then join the memory of that decision and the feelings accompanying it to your new message so that when you say your revised statement to yourself, you will connect with the positive feelings. You'll need quiet time and space to accomplish this union, but in joining a previous experience and its positive feelings with your new message, you can create a powerful combination for change.

Once the connection between the previous, positive experience and the new message is established, you are ready to reprogram your belief about yourself as someone who makes good money decisions. Write your new statement on notecards and place them everywhere—in your wallet, on the steering wheel of your car, on mirrors, in drawers you frequently open, on the refrigerator door. The idea is to be able to see them often throughout the day. Speak the statement out loud, especially standing in front of the mirror while making eye contact with yourself. Remember to recall those positive decision-making feelings.

Any time you experience a shock or surprise during the day, repeat your new belief over and over. Something as simple as a paper cut or a stubbed toe can be an opportunity for reinforcing your new message. When these kinds of surprises occur, the brain's logical processes, the ones that want to hold onto the old belief, are muted. So, when you repeat your new belief during these times, you have a better chance of embedding them in the subconscious. After a while, your subconscious accepts the new belief, allowing it to override the old.

You can use this same technique with any of your explicit messages. As you become more and more aware of the messages you carry, you will come to know not only which ones you need to change, but you will also find yourself able to prioritize. Take your changes a step at a time. Work on one belief and when you have integrated it into your everyday life, you can move on to the next. Keep at it! With some conscious practice, you'll find you can change your messages.

## Indirect Messages

Remember that direct messages are the ones you hear and of which you are consciously aware. Indirect messages, on the other hand, lurk below your consciousness and thus are much more subtle. Like the maiden in our money fable, we experience the effect of these messages when we engage in certain automatic behaviors without consciously knowing why. For example, deep-seated messages about women being powerless to earn as much money as men can result in a woman sabotaging herself just as she is about to make a breakthrough in income. When we brought out this point in a workshop, one participant suddenly blurted out, "Maybe that's why I always change to a lower paying job just as I am about to get a promotion. I thought I was bored with the old job, but I think maybe I was somehow afraid of making more money and taking on more responsibility." Have you seen this happen in your workplace?

Usually, indirect messages are based on observations made unconsciously while growing up. They are formed from the implied expectations of the significant adults in our lives, particularly adult family members. When we become adults ourselves, these indirect messages influence such things as selection of mates, how we should go about getting money, how much money is "enough," where we work, and how to define family loyalty. While all of these areas can be formidable in their influence, keeping family loyalty is perhaps the most potent. It is often the hidden source of self-sabotage.

As children, we naturally want to please our parents and will try to do that. At the same time, we are keenly observing, usually unconsciously, how our parents interact with each other and with their financial situation. We are constructing our own reality. As we grow older, we want to maintain an alignment with that reality even if we have chosen to separate from our parents.

Thus we may maintain loyalty to that picture drawn for us in our original family dynamic. For example, if the family valued security above all else, we will make every attempt to be secure even if these attempts make us miserable. If the breadwinner kept the family on the financial edge, we may keep ourselves on a similar edge, leaving jobs just before we can establish a solid financial foundation for ourselves or letting our financial reserves drop to very low levels before we take action to replenish them. We may even work for companies that create a similar atmosphere regarding money.

Family loyalty also may be maintained in the exact opposite of the childhood reality. Someone brought up in a family that was always on the edge may assume the opposite stance and strive for a strong sense of financial security. In this case, that security frequently is derived from being extremely cautious with money, even to the extent of making unwise decisions. This person would probably prefer to keep most of her money in the mattress, where she knows it's safe, but will part with enough of it to put in the bank for living expenses. Any other action is looked upon as unsafe. This person is still maintaining loyalty, but in the reverse.

## Tracing the Messages Back

When we talk about indirect messages, we're going back several generations in the family dynamic. This may come as a surprise, but these subtle messages are powerful and long lasting. So, how can we make our unconscious messages conscious and begin breaking any negative influences they may have on us? A three-generation genogram can provide us with this valuable information.

Genograms have been used by family therapists since the 1970s to illustrate family patterns and relationships. This tool is designed to give access to large amounts of information in an efficient and graphic way. A genogram is a type of family tree but with one significant difference: While a family tree asks you to make connections and trace your genetic ancestors, a genogram traces your psychological connections. According to noted family therapist Monica Mc-Goldrick, "Families are full of myths and slogans about money and its role in human affairs."[6] So it is especially appropriate to use a genogram to look at your implicit money messages.

If a genogram is new to you, we think you'll find it easy to do with a few basic instructions. It takes some time, but the time you spend constructing it will be amply rewarded by the resulting insights. Here's how it works:

Allow a minimum of twenty minutes to work. You may choose to complete your genogram in several sessions to allow enough thinking time. Have plenty of space to spread your work out—you'll need it!

Gather together marking pens or crayons and several large sheets of drawing paper, or smaller sheets of typing paper that you can tape together later. Familiarize yourself with the genogram symbols that are used for clarity and consistency.

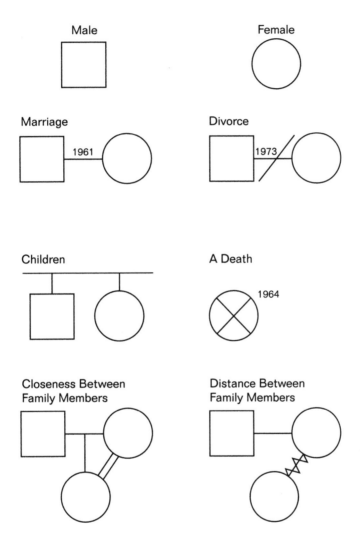

Male

Female

Marriage

1961

Divorce

1973

Children

A Death

1964

Closeness Between
Family Members

Distance Between
Family Members

With the supplies and symbols at hand, sit back, relax, and spend some time just thinking about your family. Visualize yourself and the preceding generations, giving special thought to the females in your family. Look through old family photos if that helps to put you in the right mood. Begin the genogram by drawing your generation: you, your siblings, and everyone's mates. Include divorces, deaths, stillborn children, abortions, and as much information as you can remember. Once you get started, you will probably find you remember much more than you expected to.

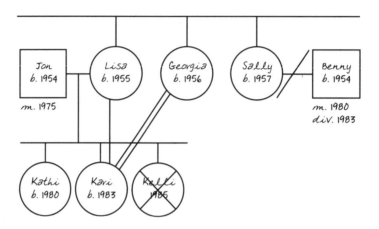

Next, work back to your mother's generation and sketch out her family. Again, be sure to include her siblings and their mates and children as you did for your own generation. Add the same information for your father's family.

Now you are ready for your grandparents. Do the same with them, again including as much information as you can remember. If you are a parent of grown children, you will probably wish to include them, as well, making a four-generation genogram. You will no doubt see patterns emerge as your children follow their understanding of family messages.

Once you have the basic information, you can fill out more of your genogram using the following suggestions. As you do this, watch for patterns.

1. List the education level and employment of family members.
2. Make a guess at the income level of family members. You may

not know exact details, but at least classify your family as to lower, middle, or upper class.

3. Jot down the ages at which people in your family married. Note divorces and the reasons, if you know them. Add in any extra-marital liaisons, out-of-wedlock children, and other pieces of information related to marriage.

4. Note the kind of men the women in your family married. You may see a pattern of ``good providers'' or the opposite, that is, men who were underemployed or couldn't hold a job. Again, list as much information as you can about common marital patterns.

5. Which family members stand out for either lower or higher income? Did anyone break a family pattern? What did they do? How did other family members regard them?

6. List the predominant family patterns you see, being especially aware of patterns for the women.

7. Note patterns of closeness and distance, and be especially aware of issues of family loyalty. How was loyalty demonstrated? Disloyalty?

8. Return to the questionnaire at the end of Chapter 1. Reread it to see if any additional patterns emerge. Also review your answers to the questions for the direct messages exercise earlier in this chapter to see if they jog any memories.

9. If you were to compose a family motto regarding money, what would it be? Write it beside your genogram.

10. Did you see any family messages that could block your success? List them as they occur to you, being as clear as you can.

11. Finally, list anything else about your family that provides information about your current money issues.

The genogram is a powerful tool for raising awareness about family issues. As you look at yours, be aware of the messages that can sabotage you in your quest for financial comfort. Note especially the roles of women in your family. Write these beside your genogram.

Here's a sample of reactions we've received from workshop participants.

> Kara (educator): "I see a pattern of women marrying men who are really 'beneath' them in education and earning power. I am aware that I have done this in my own life as well."
>
> Darlene (consultant): "The genogram helped me see why I would become so uncomfortable whenever I began to earn a high income. It felt like I was being disloyal to my father by exceeding his level and I would always do something to ensure that I never did."
>
> Megan (secretary): "Now I understand why it was so difficult for me when my husband left and I needed to get a job to support the kids. The women in my family were always supported by husbands and not expected to work outside the home. Not only did I break a pattern by divorcing, but I also broke some strong traditions of being a sheltered homemaker."

Genograms are wonderful tools because they illustrate past messages in such a clear, graphic way. Gathering this information gives you the power to take an important step toward developing a more positive relationship with money. In this case, knowledge is indeed power! We will refer back to your genogram from time to time as we progress through other money messages.

Now, let's move on to look at beliefs we picked up from society that helped to shape our perspectives toward money and its place in our lives.

# *Part Two*
# Society's Messages

*Chapter Three*

# *T*hose Sneaky Fairy Tales

Remember all those innocent fairy tales from our youth? The ones with all the happy endings. Taking a closer look at these stories reveals some of the not-so-happy messages we may have absorbed from them. These lessons have been reinforced in the novels we read and the movies and television shows we watch. What are those messages? Two of the strongest are ones we call "Coins in the Fountain" and "Money Costs . . . and Costs." Let's examine these messages and their impact on us, then explore how to get rid of them.

## Coins in the Fountain, or Wishing Makes It So

The fairy tales of our youth formed the basis for the "coins in the fountain" message that, with slight variations, continues to be updated by Hollywood and Madison Avenue. This message tells women that they don't have to bother learning about how to earn money or how to ask for what they are worth or even how to manage the money they have—a man will gladly take care of that. All we have to do is toss our coins in the fountain, wish hard enough, and our money will be taken care of.

Think of the stories we read as children. Those of us raised on *Cinderella*, *Sleeping Beauty*, *Rapunzel*, *The Frog Prince*, and similar tales know that somewhere out there is a handsome prince who will ride up and take us away from all our troubles. The famous song from the Walt Disney version of *Sleeping Beauty* says it all: "Someday My Prince Will Come."

Modern-day film versions of this message abound. In *An Officer and a Gentleman*, Debra Winger's prince literally carries her out of her assembly-line job into the happily ever after. Richard Gere plays the prince again in *Pretty Woman*, this time rescuing Julia Roberts from her life as a prostitute. The 1990s prince may have traded in his white horse for a sports car, but we are still told he'll appear. And when he does, he will know how to handle money.

The stories of our day-to-day lives convey the same message. Diane remembers a brief but pointed conversation she had with her department chair during her last semester in college. He asked her if she were engaged. When she said she wasn't, he reassured her that she would probably meet her husband in graduate school. "That's where I met my wife," he added in a comforting, "don't-you-worry-about-a-thing" tone. He never heard how dismissive he was.

So we hear this message from the media, from advertising, and even from well-intentioned colleagues. Regardless of the source, the impact remains the same. Once we buy into the belief that someone will come along and rescue us from the agony of learning how to manage money, we will convince ourselves that we don't have to bother. And we will leave ourselves vulnerable to those who say they do know how to manage money, regardless of how well they have learned or how much they actually know. As long as we're tossing our coins into the fountain and wishing for a prince to come to our rescue, we're throwing away our power.

Has this message been a part of your beliefs? It's a highly pervasive one in our culture, so it's hard to escape. It works its way into our subconscious at an early age and only a very powerful family message can counter it. This message underlies many of our depowered behaviors around money. We can conveniently ignore any aspect of our financial lives that may be uncomfortable, such as asking for a fair salary or learning about investments, if we believe we will be rescued from the discomfort.

Several women have acknowledged to us that living with a man's income made it easier for them to work without having to be concerned about how much money they made. One woman spoke for many when she said, "I'm pretty sure that if I were a man I wouldn't be content to earn $11,000–15,000 a year teaching poetry to children. I'm pretty sure I would have been more aggressive and sought a higher paying job." We're not saying that this position is inherently negative. What we are asking is that women examine the impact that this message may have had on their lives in both its positive and negative applications.

Let's look at how this lesson plays itself out when it comes to asking for what we are worth. (We examine this same issue from another perspective in Chapter 9.) If a woman buys into the belief that all she has to do is toss her coins into the fountain and wait for her prince, then she doesn't have to take responsibility for being paid what she's worth. Why bother? Mark Nelson, cofounder of OI, the world's largest career transition network, stated recently that a few years ago he conducted an informal survey of all the executive women he knew. He asked them how they arrived at their salaries. "Not a single one negotiated," he stated. "They were given a salary offer and that was that."[1]

We appreciate women's struggles with the impact of this message. Ellen, who left a lucrative career in sales to become a writer, told us, "I received a huge commission check one time and instead of celebrating my hard work, I thanked my boss for his benevolence. Like I'd had nothing to do with it!"

A cost accountant also described her conflict around being paid what she's worth: "I recently did some work for friends and had to figure out what I was worth and it was a painful exercise. I was proud of the work I did but when it came to putting a dollar value on it, I had a horrible time. It was so difficult for me that I eventually said I was willing to do the work for nothing."

Many women confided to us that they have struggled with this issue, knowing that they weren't being paid what they were worth while at the same time feeling too timid to ask for a salary more in line with their contributions. Lori, a case manager, summed up women's concerns in this area: "I find it is difficult to put a dollar amount on *me* and therefore am completely ignorant when it comes to asking what I'm worth." Similarly, a counselor stated, "Since I am never quite sure that I am good enough, putting a price tag on my worth is extremely difficult." We congratulate these women for recognizing the impact the coins in the fountain message has had on their lives.

Women also told us about facing this issue and dealing with it positively. A social worker said that as she has gotten older, knowing what she is truly worth has gotten easier. The reality of the marketplace often provides an antidote to wishing for your prince. A college administrator recalled that as she gained confidence in her ability to manage the academic departments under her control, she also gained the surety to know and ask for a salary that fit her level of expertise. One counselor flatly stated that being in private practice has helped her to ask for what she is worth. Many women told us that being the sole support of their children has forced them to resolve this issue by dealing with it in a positive, powerful way.

As long as we hold on to the hope that a prince will rescue us from having to face difficult issues like asking for what we're worth, we will stay in a depowered position. When we accept pay that is uncomfortably low, we are damaging our entire sense of self-worth. Certainly the argument can be made that our worth as individuals is not measured in dollars, but that's not what we're looking at here. Women have constantly neglected to take stock of their abilities, skills, and talents and then put a price tag on them. Yet that is the way our marketplace operates.

The woman who knows her worth as an individual and also knows her worth in a financial sense is a powerful person. She isn't wishing for some rescuing prince. Happily, we see many women moving into this mindset, ridding themselves of crippling messages. This position of strength was stated simply by Irish, an employment services specialist. About asking for what you're worth she said, "Have no problem with this. It's important to recognize your worth and ask for it."

To get in touch with any messages you may have around the coins in the fountain notion, try the following exercise:

Take a few moments to recall your favorite childhood happily-ever-after story, whether from a book, movie, television, or another source. Think about the story in its entirety. Recall it as if you were telling it to someone. Try to summon up how you felt about this story and its ending. Write those feelings here:

What beliefs did this story help you formulate? What did you believe to be true about life based on your experience with this story? Write these ideas here:

How have you acted on these beliefs throughout your life? How have they influenced your perception of events in your life? Make notes about your awareness in these areas:

Finally, what has been the result of these beliefs? How has your life been affected by them and your subsequent decisions? How do you feel about these outcomes? Make some notes about what you have realized:

• • •

For example, if you chose *Cinderella* as a favorite story, you might say that it influenced you to believe that if you worked hard—even to the point of struggling in a loveless home—eventually a man would rescue you. Gone would be the poverty of emotion and the drudgery of menial tasks, to be replaced by devoted love and attention and financial bounty.

This belief may have led you to get into relationships where you settled for less than you deserved. You may have been convinced that this was all you were entitled to, at least until you had ``suffered'' enough. You may have tolerated an unsatisfactory situation, holding the underlying belief that eventually you would be rescued. But in the end, realizing that no one was going to come to your aid, you gathered your own strength and broke out of an unhealthy situation. Now, after some soul-searching and therapy, you are more attuned to what makes a healthy relationship.

Give yourself time with this exercise. It may take a while to get insights into the influences of these early stories and beliefs. As you go through these exercises, it's important to do so nonjudgmentally.

Don't get upset with yourself if you realize that some belief you adopted in childhood has led you to decisions that you now wish had been different. Awareness is the first step in any change. That's what we want to support here—your gaining awareness regarding your relationship to money.

## *Amanda's Story*

Amanda, who was building her career in banking, kept turning down opportunities to expand her career. Her boss and coworkers finally stopped urging her to go after promotions. As she described her work, she had settled into her "comfortable niche."

In reality, she had put her career on hold, believing her fiancé would turn his life around and become the successful businessman he promised her he would be. Taking a promotion in her work would have meant Amanda would have traveled or would have had to take some risks. Each promotion would have required that she stretch herself to take on more responsibilities, make more decisions that affected other people, and make more money. Her fiancé discouraged her from moving forward, assuring her that he would make plenty of money to support her and their future children. For a long time Amanda found comfort in his words. She was willing to wait, figuring the wait would be worth it.

A friend brought Amanda to one of our workshops. Like many women, she began by saying she was only attending to keep her friend company. To her credit, she fully participated in the activities and quickly gained new insight into her relationship with both her fiancé and her money.

> I learned growing up that men were supposed to take care of women. Even though I was born several years after my parents married, I remember my mother telling me about

how she quit her job when she got married so she could provide a good home for her husband and family. I was never sure if my mother was happy about doing that or if she was just resigned to her fate. Now I realize I'm setting myself up to do the same thing—I'm putting my career and my earning power on hold while I wait for my fiancé to get his act together. I'm beginning to wonder if he's going to do that. He's had six different jobs in the last two years and I usually get stuck paying the rent.

Every time I talk about a possible promotion, he tells me he doesn't want me working after we get married. I guess I've wanted to hear that so I don't have to make any changes—take any risks. Now I see that I need to go ahead with my career and make that a priority. That way, if we do get married, I'll have that much more experience under my belt and I'll be making more money. If we break up, I'll have a well-established career and a decent income. I've been waiting for him to make good on his promises for two years. I realize I better take care of myself. I admit, though, that I feel scared when I say that. But I also feel really angry with him.

Amanda called us a couple of months later to let us know she had applied for and gotten a promotion and that she was feeling very good about taking on a new job. She also reported that while her fiancé is still in her life, she has told him he will have to move out if he quits his current job.

## Money Costs . . . and Costs

Like the coins in the fountain message, the notion that money costs and costs exists in our childhood storybooks, as well as in messages received from our family and society as a whole. This belief says that, for women, possession of wealth comes only at a very high price. When we carry this notion into our adult years, we can experience a range of emotions—from discomfort to fear to shame—over possession of wealth.

The message that money costs and costs has two parts. The first part of the message tells us that true happiness does not come from wealth. Barbara, a parent, homemaker, and part-time bookkeeper, says that one of her family messages was, "People with lots of money weren't happy." An editor says her message about wealth was, "Don't ever be flashy or think you are better than anyone else just because you have money."

As juveniles, we found our fiction filled with cautionary tales emphasizing the message that money and happiness don't go together. For example, the children's classic, *Heidi*, tells the tale of an impoverished child from a rural area who comes to the big city to be a companion to Clara, the poor little rich girl. Clara has material wealth but doesn't really know how to be happy until Heidi teaches her. Heidi eventually returns to her modest mountain life, since that is where she knows she'll be happiest, and marries Peter, a goat herder.

Similarly, the four sisters and their mother in *Little Women* have a poor but satisfying life while their father/husband is off at war. Money clearly has no place in their happiness; they are content simply with their closeness as a family. When it comes to marriage, Jo turns down a wealthy suitor, Laurie, in favor of the poor but scholarly Professor Behr. Meanwhile Meg marries the poor but hard-working Mr. Brooke. The message is clear: Poor is better and women should choose happiness over wealth since we can't have both.

The second part of the money costs and costs message tells us that our interest in money will exact a painfully high price in terms of relationships and personal happiness. We may even be punished if we get too far out of bounds with our desire for wealth. The children's tale, *The Fisherman and His Wife*, illustrates this principle. The fisherman catches a magic fish that promises to grant a wish in return for its release from the hook. After the fisherman frees the fish and is granted a modest wish, his wife repeatedly sends him back to call on the fish with additional requests, each more grand than the last. The greed eventually is punished when the fish runs out of patience and the couple loses all they have.

The movie *It Could Happen to You* presents a modern day twist to this theme. A poor police officer shares lottery winnings with a humble waitress, keeping a promise made on a day he was broke and unable to leave his usual tip. The greedy wife of the lottery winner divorces him in order to take all his money. She then marries a sleazy character who, it turns out, is only after *her* money. She loses everything because her focus was on accumulating more and more wealth, while the police officer and waitress are rewarded with riches because money was not their priority. Not only are they now wealthy, but they have also fallen in love and will no doubt live happily ever after.

Note that the greedy women in both stories have their lives ruined by their desire for money. Yet men who are motivated by money are often rewarded with fame as well as fortune. We're not judging money as a motivator—for some people it is a positive force. Our focus is on the consistently negative messages women receive about this issue. These messages put us in a box. If money happens to be a motivator for us, our role models tell us we will be greedy and unhappy. They portray lives where money and love do not go together—unless the money comes from a man. They further tell us that true happiness comes more easily to those women who do not strive for success.

We've all seen television interviews and read articles focusing on highly successful yet miserable female executives. Can you remember such a story about a man? We can't. No wonder women feel discomfort at having money and secretly question their right to a comfortable financial lifestyle. The message is clear: If we get our priorities confused and want money, we will be punished.

These pervasive messages speak to the false belief that money costs and costs. We can be wealthy and successful, the message says, but what a price we pay! Pulled between the conflicting poles of wanting money and fearing its effect on our lives, we are confused and uncertain. We see this message played out in the lives of the countless women who continually sell themselves short, don't see the value of their labor, and are willing to put in untold hours of volunteer work instead of seeking paid employment. It is demonstrated by our unwillingness to take charge of our financial lives because we have vague fears of our financial power. As Anita, an environmental scientist, aptly put it, "If you undervalue yourself, you will never catch up."

To empower ourselves, however, women need to see the flaw that lies in the either/or quality of the money costs and costs message. The old message gives us no choice. We can be wealthy and unhappy *or* we can be poor and happy. We can't have both wealth and happiness. And if we buy into this message with its accompanying negative image for professionally successful women, we are more apt to make the belief true for ourselves. For example, by believing the notion that professional success comes with a high personal-happiness price tag, a woman may unconsciously live an extreme workaholic lifestyle. She will choose a profession and a company that will financially reward her work while demanding every drop of her energy so she has nothing left for a personal life.

We propose a new message, one that gives more choices, as well as flexibility and freedom. In our workshops we have helped women to understand that life is not a forced choice exam. We can select money *and* happiness, and doing so helps us move from restrictive messages to a growth-producing lifestyle of abundance. The old fear-based messages lead to tunnel vision. We broaden our perspectives by considering the possibility that we really can have both financial comfort and happiness. As we do this, we will begin to find new role models who have empowered themselves. Karen, a nurse, stated about her relationship with money, "I think it gives me power."

The message that money costs and costs is a powerful one for women. Many women are confused by the mixed messages they have received and have fears of the hidden costs of desiring money. Through the following exercise, let's see if this message operates in your life and if it does, let's write a new, healthier message.

This exercise is designed to help you become aware of messages you may be carrying that don't belong to you and that are based on fears rather than on truth. We're going to ask you first to take a look at some of your wants concerning money. The next step is to focus on the fear that is keeping you from attaining your desired relationship to money. Here are a couple of examples of fear-based messages:

- I want to be financially successful, but I'm afraid no man will want me if I'm financially well off.
- I want to have a financially comfortable life, but I'm afraid people won't like me if I have too much money.

Now try a few sentence completions for yourself. Write them here. We suggest you do this at least three times.

I want _____,
but I'm afraid _____.
I want _____,
but I'm afraid _____.
I want _____,
but I'm afraid _____.

Now take a look at the genogram you completed in Chapter 2. Underline the fear words you find there. Who used these words?

Whom did you learn these fears from as you were growing up? To whom do these fears rightfully belong? Write that information here:

_____

_____

_____

_____

Fears about money don't come naturally to us. They are developed. Now is the time to give your fears back to the person who originally gave them to you. As before, we urge you to do this free of blaming and judgments. The purpose is to rid yourself of extraneous messages so you can develop the beliefs you want to have about money.

When the fear comes up for you, either as internal self-talk or in your behavior, remind yourself that this message is not true for you. Then mentally send it back to whoever gave you the idea to begin with. We call this ``putting it in the cosmic mail.'' Each time you reject a fear that you picked up from someone else, you allow your own Truth to have its voice.

Now imagine you have given back all your fears about money. What would your ``I want . . .'' statements look like? Try rewriting them, making the appropriate shift in wording. For example:

- I want to be financially successful **and** I enjoy the freedom that having my own money gives me.
- I want to have a financially comfortable life **and** I enjoy the feelings I have from living without worrying about money.

Now try rewriting the sentences you wrote earlier:

I want _____

and I enjoy _____.

I want _____

and I enjoy _____.

I want _____

and I enjoy _____.

How do you feel as you read over the new versions? Say them out loud to give them another, even more powerful dimension. If you feel safe, read them to a friend who will just listen, without commenting. Reclaiming your voice concerning money takes time and vigilance, but the rewards are bountiful.

## Vera's Story

Vera told us about how her childhood deeply impacted on her life decisions. One of seven children of an alcoholic mother and a hard-working but usually absent father, she experienced early on the difficulties of living on a shoestring budget. Because she was the oldest, her father insisted she have a paper route when she turned thirteen. She remembers the thrill of having her own money and decided with her first pay that she wanted a lot more. Working through high school and college, Vera became more determined to be successful.

She consciously chose a career in commission sales because she knew her income possibilities were unlimited. Before she reached her thirties, she had a six-figure income with all the accompaniments. We met her in her mid-forties. Now highly respected in her field, she was a sophisticated, well-traveled woman who appeared to have it all.

But she told us what she felt was missing and why:

I haven't realized until now that when I decided to be so successful I also told myself I would have to go it alone. That a man would be intimidated by such success. I mean, that was what we believed—a woman couldn't have both a successful career and a stable relationship. I didn't know how deeply I believed that.

Now I understand what I've been doing to myself with this either/or belief. I've been dating someone for about six months and I've been experiencing a lot of new feelings. I usually date people who are essentially unavailable—I realized a while back that I do this so I won't have to make a commitment. I don't want to do that anymore, so now I'm in a different kind of relationship and I find myself holding back. Unconsciously I've been keeping distance because I believe that if I truly commit to a strong, primary relationship, I'll have to give up my level of success. I don't really know if that's true or not. I've just been acting as if it were. I'd like to explore the possibility that my message doesn't have to be true. And I think I've found the right person to explore with.

## Chapter Four

# *Taking Your Power Back*

Most of us who have come through the "feminist revolution" of recent decades think of ourselves as strong, independent individuals. We understand that we have choices and we take responsibility for our decisions. We certainly don't want to believe that we might put ourselves into a dependent relationship with money. As with other troublesome yet subtle messages we have examined, we ask you to consider the possibility. In this chapter, we're first going to explore the dependent relationship with money that society encourages women to have. Then we look at the equally depowering message that meek is better. And we suggest ways to heal these damaging beliefs.

## Women in the Dependent Role

Women assume a dependent relationship with money when they approach their money dealings from three basic beliefs:

- I shouldn't have to.
- I don't want to.
- I can't.

According to Ruth Hayden, a financial planner who teaches money management classes for women, these are the beliefs she most often encounters in her work with women.[1] In reality, these beliefs are a surefire formula for life in the dependent role.

How did we learn dependency? Why do we let it perpetuate? Most important, what can we do to change it? All of the societal money messages we have discussed, as well as our family messages, contribute to this stance. Many women have learned how to be helpless where money is concerned, to give their power away by avoiding responsibility and burying their heads in the sand. Or they have spent too much time waiting for the prince. While many of these messages came to us in subtle ways, some were delivered more directly.

For example, some of us have received a message that says money equals love. This is a controlling attitude that tells an individual, "You know I love you because I buy you things." Material goods take the place of love. A gift does not *symbolize* love as it does in a healthier situation, rather, it becomes a *substitute* for love. An adult carrying this belief has many challenges in dealing with both money and intimate relationships. She may stay financially dependent on her parents because a steady flow of money means that they love her. Or she may constantly demand more materially from her partner so she can believe she is loved.

Additionally, this person may fail to understand why her gifts are not accepted by others in place of genuine caring. With love and money so entwined, losing a money connection to another person also means losing the love of that individual. This belief results in an unhealthy, dependent relationship with money as well as unhealthy relationships with other people.

While our old messages may tempt us, even to the point of giving us permission to withdraw from dealing with our financial affairs and remain dependent, being dependent is an unhealthy choice. Today we can no longer fall into the dependency role and allow ourselves the luxury of ignoring the financial realities facing us. Women have made great strides in achieving equal opportunities with men in the business world. Yet the fact remains that the only two professions in which women outearn men are modeling and prostitution. In the rest of the career world, women currently can expect to earn 71 cents for every dollar earned by men. Not only do women earn less, but they also have fewer years in the workforce because of family responsibilities, and thus have less time to accumulate retirement funds.

The picture gets downright scary when we look at older women as a group. Estimates tell us that by the year 2000, 19 *million* American women will lack adequate pension funds.[2] Women are more likely to end up alone and living at poverty level than are men in the same age group.[3] We don't want these projections to come true.

Divorce can substantially harm a women's financial prospects because it hits women harder than it does men. Most women will experience a greater drop in standard of living than do men. Further, women tend not to receive adequate spousal or child support, or if they do, many experience great difficulty in collecting it.[4]

This is, indeed, disconcerting information. Of even greater concern is the fact that many women have difficulty assuming responsibility for their future. Thirty-seven percent of American women spend no time in financial planning.[5] Two recent surveys conducted by mutual fund companies indicate that women are becoming more savvy about investing and are more willing to take risks than they were five years ago.[6] We hope this trend among women investors spreads to the rest of the population. We want to see 100 percent of American women actively engaged in planning their financial futures.

Dependency becomes a self-fulfilling prophecy. Women who believe they are not in control of their financial lives don't plan adequately for retirement. And they are neither surprised nor angry when financial institutions ignore them—that's what they expect. Widowhood or divorce leaves them in dire financial straits. Being dependent even gives them license to continue in their helpless ways as they say, "Someone should help me." They also risk buying into the self-fulfilling prophecy of "I can't, and even if I do, it won't make any difference."

We have two choices: continuing in the fear-based mode or choosing a more powerful means of coping. We urge women to reject the dependent mentality with all its subtle manifestations and operate from a position of self-knowledge and personal power. Now is the time to rewrite this damaging message and take control of our financial lives!

Looking at the money messages we carry from the past gives us the power to rewrite them for the present, which, in turn, gives us control over our future. One woman summed up this dynamic nicely when she said, "I am challenged as an adult to throw out the childhood messages and replace them with new ones, because the old messages are dangerous for me to live by any longer." We encourage you to accept the same challenge.

Moving out of dependent thinking requires a strong sense of self. While women have traditionally been good at nurturing strength in others, we have had trouble nurturing ourselves. The following exercise is designed to help you move toward a stronger sense of self.

Think about your strengths. What are you good at? Focus on the things that are rewarding for you and that may even be quite easy for you to do. Our strongest assets are often natural gifts and talents that we tend to overlook. List at least three strengths here:

1. _____
2. _____
3. _____

You may want to enlist the help of a friend who can tell you what strengths she sees in you. Often we can overlook what is obvious to someone else.

Now, taking each strength in turn, close your eyes, and, saying it out loud, see yourself using this ability. Be as vivid as you can. Let yourself feel throughout your body what using this strength feels like.

What do you notice? Often people sit up straighter than they usually do. Their bodies relax so energy moves more freely. Get up and move around, feeling your strength. Practice walking from a place of strength. People generally move differently when they do this. Shoulders come back in a relaxed position. The head is erect instead of leaning forward. People walk in a more balanced way—they're centered and more fluid in their motions. What do you notice as you walk from a position of strength?

Let these feelings sink into your body. Remind yourself of these sensations as you walk and move. Being helpless and moving from a position of strength are incompatible. The choice is yours.

## Sandra's Story

Sandra stayed at home, raising her children and focusing her energies on helping her husband build his career. As her children needed her less and less, she decided to return to college and complete her education. She had spent many hours as a volunteer in her children's school and had always thought teaching would be a good career. Her working hours would match her children's hours and she would be home in plenty of time to fix a good meal every night.

After six months in college, Sandra was feeling more stress than she had ever felt. She thought she should have been happy—everyone told her she had made a good decision. Her children and husband supported her decision and were even helping out around the house. This should have been a satisfying, stimulating time in her life, yet she felt increasingly uneasy. She decided to talk with a career counselor at the college. During this discussion, the counselor asked about her interests and the coursework she enjoyed most. Sandra told her how much she was enjoying her algebra class. So much, in fact, that she found working algebraic equations to be very relaxing.

The more she talked about her interest in math, the more the counselor urged her to consider a career that would allow her to use her strengths. At first, Sandra interpreted this suggestion to mean she should teach math. The counselor asked her why she was so intent on teaching and Sandra stated her logical reasons. At the same time, she realized that she loved math, not the idea of teaching math.

After doing some research, Sandra discovered the many math-related careers open to her.

> I was getting very excited about all the possibilities that were beginning to open to me. Yet every time I would think about actually changing my major, my stomach would turn. I hadn't talked about my ideas with anyone in my family. I was afraid they would be upset by my having an eight-hour a day job. I worried about what my children would do if I wasn't home when they got home from school. Finally, I worked up the nerve to approach them. To my surprise, they thought the idea was great. My oldest son pointed out that by the time I finished with my degree he would be a senior, ready to graduate, and the others would be old enough to look after themselves for a couple of hours. My husband just said he wanted me to be happy.
>
> I was relieved after our talk, but I think I was a little disappointed, too. They didn't need me as much as I thought they did. Still, the next day I formally changed my major and am now working my way to becoming a CPA. As time has gone by, I realize that my family does need me, just not in ways they used to.

## Meek Is Better

What contradictions modern women face. We have, as the cigarette ad says, come a long way. Women have been elected to high political offices, held important executive positions, served as faculty members and administrators at colleges and universities, and generally achieved goals our great-grandmothers only dreamed of. And yet, there remains a part of many accomplished women that is uncomfortable with accomplishments and questions their right to strive and achieve. The niggling fear that these women are risking being labeled "unladylike" picks at success and makes the message that "meek is better" a strong one.

The meek is better message lays down guidelines about how women should behave. It tells us we must not be strong or more independent or smarter than the men in our lives. It tells us we should soft-pedal our talents and abilities and defer to the people who we believe are more knowledgeable. Meek, ladylike behavior is held up as an ideal. This message pervades our society. Like the coins in the fountain message, meek is better came to us through the fiction we read, the movies and television we watched, and the role models we observed. We read fairy tales in which the heroine needed to be rescued by the stronger, more capable man. We saw Sleeping Beauty awakened by the kiss of the prince and Red Ridinghood rescued in the nick of time by the brave huntsman. Our childhood fiction helped us learn our roles as did the television we watched while growing up. We saw men portrayed as more active, women as more passive. Even the voice-overs selling products were male. In our growing-up years, the boys in our schoolbooks were the actors, the girls usually sat on the sidelines and cheered.[7]

We carry these messages telling us that meek is better into our daily lives. In her book *Schoolgirls* Peggy Orenstein interviewed numerous girls who made the choice to hang back and not show their academic ability for fear of being seen as too smart and thus undesirable to boys.[8] These girls are learning to defer to the men in their lives, thus buying into meek is better.

Our grown-up role models demonstrate their own brand of "meek." Barbara Bush, clearly a bright, capable woman, winds up on

America's list of most admired women not for her individual accomplishments, but for her support of her husband's presidency. Nancy Reagan's task as first lady and ex-first lady is to care for and support her husband. But when other first ladies such as Eleanor Roosevelt and Hilary Clinton take an active role in their husband's presidencies or have power in their own right, we as a nation become suspicious of their motives.

To reinforce the importance of staying meek, we are told that financial success on our own is unfeminine. In that regard, the stereotype of the rich dragon lady persists. Leona Helmsley is reputed to have said that paying taxes is for "the little people." Many men have made similar remarks over the years, but because of our society's prejudices against women having independent wealth, we are more likely to remember Helmsley's comment rather than a similar one from a man. Remember the public anger toward Helmsley and contrast that with the milder outcry over Charles Keating's alleged misdeeds. Wealthy, powerful women appear to make us much more uncomfortable than their male counterparts.

The women who responded to our questionnaire addressed the conflict many of us feel when we are caught in the "meek is better" message. Barbara articulated the dilemma for many women when she said, "Making money is difficult or uncomfortable for me. I have a hard time doing it and when I do I often feel underpaid." Shirley, a business owner, told us, "I am more comfortable giving than receiving." Jeanne, an art instructor, related that in her relationship, "I saw my role as comforter, homemaker for the 'breadwinner.' I saw the acquisition of goods as fraught with difficulty and *the* goal of work was to get ahead."

The meek is better message keeps us from achieving our potential in the financial world. Not only will we play out this message by not asking for raises we know we've earned, but we will also join a company that encourages us to play out the meek is better message. The organizational culture may be a patriarchal, patronizing one in which women's ideas are dismissed. Glass ceilings make up an integral part of the architecture. Whatever the message, there will always be an organization willing to play it out.

The meek is better message also has huge implications for our self-esteem. Since true self-esteem is derived from and built on what we accomplish in our lives, failure to achieve our potential is bound to have an effect on our view of ourselves.[9] The "Little Miss Meek" role is one fraught with negative consequences for women. We don't learn to take charge of our own affairs and, if we do happen to achieve success, confusion and discomfort result, not celebration.

Unless we begin to understand that we no longer have to be passive but can set our own goals, we will continue to feel torn as we wait for a provider to take care of us. Further, women will remain in a depowered position. We can achieve self-esteem only on our own—no one can give it to us. Thus, having to pin our inner worth on someone else's accomplishments leaves us on shaky ground in terms of self-confidence and self-esteem.

Has the meek is better message been part of your life? Let's see how it operates and how it can be changed by participating in the following exercise:

This exercise is designed to help you become aware of your accomplishments, regardless of their size. Women tend to dismiss their successes, particularly the ones that society also fails to recognize. When we ask people to talk about their accomplishments, they often look for the big things. If they can't find them, they conclude there are no successes to acknowledge. We want to stretch this notion of achievement and help you recognize and celebrate your efforts.

Make a list of three accomplishments or successes you have had. Perhaps you feel good about returning to school after a long hiatus. Or maybe you went to the dentist alone for the first time. Perhaps you remember giving a speech in eighth grade that terrified you but you did it anyway. When these happened is not important—one might be within the last week, another might be from your childhood. Neither is its size important. Don't get tripped up by society's definition of success. We're asking for something you did that required a special effort on your part or that you felt especially good about. Whether or not anyone else was aware of the accomplishment is irrelevant.

Write down what you can remember about the event. How did you feel about it? Did you take responsibility for the success or try to give it to someone else or even dismiss it? Did you tell others about it? Did you get recognition from others? How did you feel about that?

Now read your description out loud. Come up with some way that you can reward yourself for each accomplishment. What can you do to celebrate yourself as an individual who is successful? It's important to mark these events for yourself rather than hope someone else will notice. And it's important to take in the positive energy of the success celebration. Each time you do this, you are nurturing your innate strengths and becoming a more powerful individual.

The meek is better message helped women learn to hang back and not strive for success on our own. Further, for many women, it taught us to go underground with our strengths and derive our satisfaction from supporting someone else. This message has damaging effects on women's assessment of our abilities to manage our financial affairs, and has lead us to fear rather than welcome the opportunity to take charge of our financial lives. Getting in touch with our version of "Little Miss Meek" and other messages that encourage dependency is a major leap forward in regaining control over our financial lives.

## *Alice's Story*

Alice was a vibrant woman in her mid-seventies. She told us she didn't think she had any money issues, but she just liked coming to personal growth workshops. We watched as she diligently drew her genogram and noticed that she had had several husbands. During the discussion that followed, she began explaining that she married right out of high school. Her first husband was killed in an automobile accident. A year later, she remarried. This union only lasted a few years, ending in divorce. She stayed single for a while, finding work in a factory. She married a third time. Ten years later, at the age of forty-two, she lost her husband to cancer. She retired from her factory job at sixty-five, having enjoyed her single life.

As she talked about her life and marriages, she suddenly stopped talking. Her eyes widened, filling with tears as she blurted out, "I haven't had a name of my own for almost my whole life!" We waited as this realization sunk in and she began making her adjustment to this revelation. "I gave up my name and a little piece of who I was every time I married. I thought that was what I was supposed to do. No wonder I enjoyed being single! I wonder what else besides my name I have given up." We didn't need to suggest that perhaps she had given up many aspects of her personal power, including financial, during her marriages. Clearly, she would make that discovery on her own.

*Chapter Five*

# *T*hose Sneaky Fears

We've heard it said that we are worried about money to the extent that we don't have it! The time has come to put our energy-draining money concerns to rest so we can use that energy to construct a healthier relationship with money. Society has given us plenty of messages connecting money and security that play into our fears rather than building confidence. The best way to deal with any fear is head-on, so that's what we'll do here—look at the ties between money and security, and then face the nasty, pervasive "I could become a bag lady" fear.

## Money = Security

For most people, separating money and security is difficult. So in looking at the money = security message, we realize we are tackling a fundamental belief. While both sexes get this message, the women's version in particular urges us to find a good provider and stick with him at all costs. In the broader discussion of all of society's messages, this belief comes under the category "any relationship is better than no relationship."

Women in our workshops have made some strong statements in discussing what they are willing to trade off for security. Here are a few examples:

"I don't acknowledge his [her husband's] infidelity. I'd rather have the financial security than leave, so I just pretend it isn't happening."

"Sure, her husband was unfaithful, but he made it up to her. Their house was a showplace and she always had the best of everything. It's not a great life but at least she is compensated for her suffering."

"The drinking is sometimes a problem, but for the most part he makes a good living. I would hate to be a single parent and raise the kids on my own. For me, staying is better than leaving."

"We really don't have much in common now, and maybe we never did. It's just too hard for me to start over at my age, and I'm comfortable with our financial lifestyle, so I just close my eyes and put up with things as they are."

"Sure my job is demanding. I know I'm stressed. But the pay is good and I really need the benefits."

The money = security message, like the others we have discussed, has its roots in our childhood and adolescence. The majority of the women in our survey reported that, for their mothers especially, this message was pervasive. We watched our mothers be fearful of not having enough money for security and learned to be fearful ourselves. Further, the message that came across clearly was that earning money rested in the hands of men while women were only the managers of household expenses. Regarding her mother's messages, Jeanne, an art instructor, said, "It was to be the husband's role to get out in the marketplace—the home was centered around the father as all powerful and all important." For Lori's mother the message was "Security is being married to my husband." A business owner told us that she saw her mother's messages as, "Security is a husband with a profitable business. I am a kept woman."

The money = security message is difficult to deal with because it is rooted in our family history. Years ago, most women *had* to make the best of a bad marriage. They simply had no choice, so the best part of the trade-off seemed to be hanging onto that proverbial good provider. As an eighty-year-old respondent said, "When we girls married, Mother told us to be sure that this was what we wanted to do because once we left home we could not come back again. If we made our beds, we would have to lie on them forever."

The money = security message also touches some of our deep-seated fears. It is closely related to what may be the ultimate fear for most women, the "I Could Become a Bag Lady" message to be addressed later in this chapter. Are we advocating that all of the women previously quoted leave their partners and immediately strike out on their own? No, of course not. Nor are we suggesting women ignore financial dangers lurking in the real world. We have only to read the statistics about women and poverty to see that our fears have a basis in reality. We do hope, however, that women will take a clear-headed look at their lives.

The belief that money can buy security is an illusion for several reasons. First, security based on another individual is fleeting. Women who pin their security on a husband's income are ignoring what therapists call the 3-D risks of married life: divorce, disability, and death. Any of the three can lead to a drastic change in fortunes, and unless a woman is prepared, she can find herself without the security she so prized. What if the unfaithful husband decides to end the marriage during one of his flings? How about the problem drinker who has a drunk driving accident and ends up disabled?

The money = security message can also play itself out in our working lives. Just as some women stay in unhealthy primary relationships believing that they are gaining security, some women stay in unhealthy work situations for the same reason. The relationship we have with work can be fraught with the same misconceptions that led to the same emotional desert as our personal relationships. This attitude supports workers who watch their colleagues getting laid off while denying that they are next in line. They feel exempt from the Department of Labor's pronouncement that the average U.S. worker can expect to be laid off seven times in his or her working lifetime. Equating money with security on the job is just as hazardous as it is in one's personal life.

Life is so uncertain; all we really have to count on is the present. Selling ourselves for the illusion of security rarely brings happiness and usually not even the much-prized security. We know this instinctively, and yet we can continue to ignore our wiser Self for the mistaken goal of security. True security can be found only within ourselves.

Second, the money = security belief exacts a terrible price. Women who put their emotions in the deep freeze to make do in a bad relationship, whether personal or professional, run the risk of realizing too late that the sacrifices they made came with a high price. The infamous "golden chain" metaphor that we have heard employees use illustrates how the money = security notion operates on the job. Workers who feel trapped in a job they hate say they are held by golden chains—the pay and benefits. "I would lose too much if I leave now" is a statement we have frequently heard. Thus, people remain in a job that has lost its challenge and growth potential as prisoners of fear. Chronic depression frequently results. Sometimes, too, a physical price is paid. Because our minds and bodies are so intimately connected, unhappiness often manifests itself in a physical symptom. Migraine headaches, fatigue, backaches, asthma, allergies, eating disorders, and a host of other ailments can be the body's way of telling us that something in our way of living needs to change.

Third, true security cannot be purchased with money. Security comes from knowing who we are and what is important to us. It comes from trusting ourselves to make good choices and survive if we make bad ones. We carry true security with us wherever we go as an inner source of strength. Too much focus on money leaves us unbalanced emotionally and spiritually. Marilyn, an independent sales manager, put it aptly when she observed, "Security is an illusion. The only security is trusting and accepting change."

An important part of understanding how our past money messages affect present-day behaviors is to examine carefully how we equate money with security. To help yourself deal with these fear-based messages, try the following exercise:

Refer back to your genogram to get in touch with how you learned to be fearful in regard to money. Whose voice(s) do you hear when you think about these fears? What did the person say? Be as specific as possible. Write your answers here:

_____

_____

_____

_____

Using your imagination, visualize the person giving you this message. See the person as clearly as you can, visualizing clothing, body language, and facial expression. Hear in your mind the tone of the voice and the words.

Now see yourself returning the message to the sender. You may wish to visualize yourself handing the message back to its originator or mailing it back in an envelope stamped in big red letters, ``Return to Sender.'' As you return the message tell yourself, ``I know now what they didn't. I allow myself to return these fears that do not belong to me and that serve no purpose in my life today.''

This is a powerful opportunity to free yourself of old messages that don't fit who you are today. Practice this exercise as many times as you need to with as many family members as appropriate. Some fears may be relatively new in the family while others may go back several generations. Appreciate that you are breaking patterns and give yourself lots of time with this exercise. Realize that ridding yourself of these fears requires vigilance. One by one, you will begin to see changes in your belief system as evidenced by your new behaviors.

The money = security messages are indeed strong ones. By consciously disconnecting the two, we can move toward a more balanced approach to both our financial and our personal relationships. This balance enables us to make choices from a position of strength not fear. We are free to view money for what it is, a tool that, if used properly, contributes to our physical, emotional, and spiritual well-being. Relationships, too, become a choice rather than necessary for survival when viewed from this balanced perspective. We chose to enter all our relationships because they enhance what we already have going for us. What a freeing concept! What a positive, growth-enhancing choice!

## I Could Become a Bag Lady

Lots of studies have shown us that women are terrific worriers. With fear as the motivator, most of us are highly skilled at worrying about events that are unlikely to happen, but we're still afraid they might. The greatest fear expressed repeatedly on our questionnaire and in our workshops is the fear of becoming a "bag lady." We worry about losing our financial resources as well as our ability to work and provide for our families and ourselves.

This obsession is a relatively recent phenomenon in our culture, but it seems to be taking hold. However, as we worry about a possibly disastrous future, we burn up a lot of energy that could be used to move us in a positive direction financially.

Our money questionnaire gave us variations on the bag lady theme, with women expressing the following fears:

"Homelessness."

"I won't be able to take care of myself and my family."

"Losing my children and our home is my greatest, deepest, darkest fear."

"I will lose my home and be trapped in poverty when I'm elderly."

"I will become dependent on others and burden others."

"I will have to depend on the government to support me."

The sight of a homeless woman pushing her belongings in a shopping cart can evoke a "That could be me!" reaction. There is a realistic basis for this kind of fear. We have been told by "experts" that women are one man away from welfare. We see homeless people begging on our street corners and sleeping in our alleyways. Those of us who had parents who lived through the Great Depression or suffered any other traumatic loss of financial stability probably have heard about or remember the hard times that followed.

Our family messages can set the stage for the bag-lady fear. Women who grew up in families for whom there had been a reversal of fortune are aware of the strength and pervasiveness of this message. Jeanne told us, "My parents struggled through the Depression years as parents of a growing family. One must work hard." A college student told us that in her family, "Money was very hard to get; one had to work extremely hard for it. I saw it as a thing to worry about." A counselor stated her messages as, "There's never enough; hunger hurts."

Extreme fears of losing financial security can also come from growing up in families in which money is used as a method of control. "Everything had a price tag: grades, chores, good behavior, looking pretty on Easter," according to one respondent. And just as money is given, money can be taken away. Instead of having funds because we are part of a family and thus entitled to share in the resources, money can be used as punishment and control. Some of us learned that there was not enough to go around and that what there was, was dependent on good behavior. Lisa, a counselor, said that her message was "Spending is OK only if you have been good." The resulting anxiety from this message leads many women to mistrust and worry about their ability to provide for themselves.

Money as a taboo subject in our family of origin also may have contributed to our adult fears. We learned early on that it was not OK to ask how much money our parents made. A counselor told us, "How much my dad made was nobody's business, including mine." An editor said that in her family money was "unspoken. We never acknowledged it." When money, like sex, was an unsuitable subject for discussion, many women were left in the dark about its proper place in their lives.

Marriage counselors list conflicts over money as one of the major issues bringing couples to marital therapy. Most of us, however, knew this fact intuitively before we read any of the studies on conflict in marriage. Some watched our parents fight about money and even lie about it to each other. Ellen told us that in her family "money tended to be the source of anxiety. My parents were always tight about it, and it seemed from my mother's perspective there was never enough." In discussing her parents' views on money, Susan, a consultant, gave her mother's message as, "When I spend money, never tell your father about it. Your father is cheap. It is better to withhold information or lie about money spent than to get into a fight about it." Lisa said her mother saw it "as a way husbands control wives." A business owner related that her mother was "out of the loop as far as our family finances." "Mother had to ask for every penny; father hid money in his desk," stated another woman.

Watching our parents struggle with their money issues set us up to be uncertain and unclear when it comes to our adult relationship with money. We have seen the problems and want to avoid them in our financial lives, but don't know how. Our family lives didn't prepare us to do so and our mixed messages keep us off balance. Does this dilemma sound familiar?

The bag-lady fear affects the majority of women we surveyed. The debilitating effect this message has on our ability to be comfortable with money keeps us from a logical approach to financial security. Dealing with the fear is important as we separate out childhood issues from current realities. When we are in a fear-based position, we react to present-day events with a childhood mentality. We must keep a constant check on reality as we remind ourselves that "that was then, this is now."

Coping with fear-based messages can be challenging, which is why we address this issue several times throughout this book. It demands truth. At the same time, facing fears is extremely empowering. Each time we name a fear and face it with our Truth, we take power away from the fear and reclaim that power for ourselves. With persistence, our behaviors are no longer fear driven and become much healthier.

When we conjure up our worst-case scenario around any issue, we are doing what's known as catastrophizing. In other words, we're making a catastrophe where none currently exists. We dredge up our deepest fear, see ourselves wallowing in it, and stop there. In reality, life goes on. But when we are catastrophizing, we forget that fact. We look only at the fear, never at what happens next. When this happens, we've put ourselves into a depowered position, giving the fear our power. The way to reclaim our power in this situation is to face the fear and either rid ourselves of it or follow it to its logical outcome. The following exercise helps you do just that:

Using a separate sheet of paper, complete the following sentences:

I worry most about _____
_____.

My greatest money fear is _____
_____.

The worst thing that could happen financially is _____
_____.

To rid yourself of these fears, you can do any of several things with what you've written. Take stock of your emotional relationship to each of your statements before deciding what to do. What may be appropriate in one case may not be in another—use your judgment.

One way to rid yourself of these statements is to *literally* get rid of them by dissolving the paper in water, throwing it in the trash, burying it in the dirt, or burning it. In the case of burning the paper, affirm as you watch it burn that you are releasing the fear, literally watching it change from one form of energy into another. Or you may want to tear the paper into pieces and simply throw it away. Shredding it may give you more of a sense of releasing the fear energy. Some people even find it appropriate to flush the tiny pieces down the toilet. Whatever you chose to do, allow the fear feelings to be released with your action.

Another way to gain a more powerful perspective about your fears is to carry them beyond the basic statement. Look at your sentences again. Pick one, read it over, then answer the question, What happens next? After you have responded, answer the same question again. And again, and again. Keep doing that, extending the fear image as far as you can go. For example, suppose you have written, "My greatest money fear is losing all I have." What happens next? "After I lose all my money, I have to move in with family." What happens next? "I get a job flipping hamburgers." What happens next? "After six months I'm ready to go nuts from all those hamburgers so I get a job in an office." What happens next? Well, you get the point.

The bag-lady fear can be a difficult one to confront. It is pervasive and powerful. Because it lurks in our imagination, it has the power to take hold of us when we are most vulnerable. It assumes a life of its own as we give it the energy to grow. By bringing it to our consciousness, we can combat it with a major dose of reality, thus freeing ourselves from its effects.

Our fears can become larger than they deserve to be and can

take a lot of power because we neglect to realize that life goes on. Seeing our fears from this perspective can help us realize they are not so big after all.

## *Francis's Story*

Sometimes our workshop participants give us wonderful insights about how to handle stumbling blocks. Fran told us about how she coped with several of her money fears. A woman in her mid-forties, she successfully raised two children after her husband left. In spite of her successes in maintaining a family and a home, she still carried her share of worries. An unstable childhood left her with the money = security message, and witnessing the burgeoning growth of the homeless during the 1980s combined to bring her fears to the surface. Accumulated sleepless nights brought on by images of pushing a cart that held all her belongings led her to the realization that she needed to face her fear head-on. After writing about her dilemma in her journal, she realized how paralyzing her worries had become. As she relayed her resolution to us:

> I finally just looked at myself in the bathroom mirror and said, "Look, Fran, if you're going to be homeless, why not prepare for it so you can stop worrying about it." So I got out a grocery bag and filled it with everything I thought I would need if I were suddenly thrown out onto the street— toothbrush and toothpaste, sturdy walking shoes, extra socks, warm sweater, a change of clothes, soap, deodorant, a pillow, blanket, and some cash. I realized that I really didn't need all that much stuff. Anyway, I put everything into the bag and put the bag into the back of my closet. And I reminded myself anytime the bag-lady fear cropped up that I was prepared. In a very short time, I quit worrying about it. What a relief! Putting that worry aside has given me a lot more energy to deal with my *real* issues about money.

# Part Three
## Personal Attitudes

*Chapter Six*

# $\mathscr{T}$he Treadmill to Nowhere: Money as an Addiction

How many people do you know who belong to a health club? Perhaps you're a member of one. Working out in a gym is certainly a common way to stay fit. As more and more people commit to getting healthy, the variety of exercise equipment has increased. Treadmills, stationary bicycles, rowing machines, stair-climbing machines, even cross-country skiing machines have found an audience. Regardless of which piece of equipment we pick, however, the effect is the same: we stress, sweat, push our heart rates to the max, and go nowhere. We work harder and harder only to stay in one spot! So it is with obsessive and addictive behaviors—much activity without any forward movement.

We're not knocking sensible exercise—both of us have broken a sweat for our health. Our point is that routines involving money and exercise can be viewed in a similar way. If we have a realistic understanding of what both can do for us, and are moderate and sensible in their pursuit, money and exercise work to our benefit. If we get out of balance, either one can become addictive and thus, would no longer be positive forces in our lives. Becoming addicted to money is a personal attitude that puts us on an unhealthy treadmill to nowhere.

Does money really qualify as an addiction? Can women become

addicted to pursuing and holding onto money? The answer to both questions is yes. Addiction happens when someone becomes habitually devoted to something and cannot give it up without a struggle. People become addicted to money just as they become addicted to food, drugs, or alcohol. Looking at this addiction is a necessary step in helping us clarify our money issues and learn more positive ways of coping.

Money is a curious force in our lives. We lust after it, fight over it, marry for it, inherit it, steal it, hoard it, counterfeit it, avoid it. Sigmund Freud told us that our early toilet training influences how and why we spend or save money. A retired consultant told us about being bribed by her mother—use the potty and get a pair of roller skates. The ploy worked, but the woman lamented that the experience "formed the basis of my life and relationship with money for the next forty years." Furthermore, the presence or absence of money can color our worldview, make us happy, worried, suspicious, angry, competitive, secure, or frustrated.

With all of this activity around money, it's no wonder that we frequently lose sight of the fact that money gets value from standards established by a government. Without this value, money as a physical object would be worthless. There is nothing sacred about our current form of coins and greenbacks; earlier societies used shells, trading beads, or other items that were perceived as valuable in their life context. If we lived in a society in which everything could be had for bartering services, our dollars would be worth nothing and services would take an honored place instead.

In reality, money is merely a medium of exchange. We, along with the society in which we live, give money its value. And when we invest it with emotional meaning, we give it power over us. This knowledge can be simultaneously scary and freeing. We need to look at the position we have given money in our lives to see if it is healthy or unhealthy. If our focus on money has become so all consuming that it qualifies as an addiction, the time has come to make some changes.

How often have you heard the cliche "Money is the root of all evil"? Probably more times than you can count. If we trace the quote back to its original source in the Bible, however, we find something interesting. The actual quotation reads, *"The love of* money is the root of all evil" (emphasis added). Quite a difference! Why has this misquotation wormed its way into our culture? We believe it reflects our tendency to confuse money as an *object* with money as *a means to an end*. In other words, we give money a value that exists only in our minds. It really isn't money that gives us problems; it's our attitude toward it. And this attitude gives money its potentially addictive nature. Here's how two women illustrated this confusion:

> "Money is evil! But necessary."
> "Money is a pain in the ass, angst-producing. Lucky I've got it so I can start my own business."

These comments illustrate a truth about money that characterizes other addictions as well. If we are addicted to something, whether it is food, alcohol, drugs, relationships, or money, we have a love–hate relationship with it. Further, we spend an inordinate amount of time thinking about how we will obtain this coveted object. We won't be happy once we do acquire it, however, because that is the circular nature of addiction. We attain what we seek, but instead of taking time to enjoy it, we must immediately begin to think about how we'll get the next "fix."

This is the pattern of addiction: We are not happy without it, but once we get it, we are still not particularly happy. Further, because we are so focused on the acquisition of our desire, we neglect ourselves and our relationships in the process. We may even compromise ourselves in the work setting, sticking with jobs that are not satisfying because of an addiction to a particular size paycheck. It truly becomes a no-win situation. We are confused and unable to keep our focus on what is really important. How did we end up this way? Let's look at a few possibilities.

Somewhere along the way, our modern society has developed a misplaced focus on acquiring money for its own sake instead of as a means to ensure our survival. We look with envy at the Donald Trumps and Bill Gateses of today. We read magazines and attend workshops that claim to be able to help us emulate their success. To become rich is the American dream. At the same time, we take collective satisfaction when some financial catastrophe befalls one of the wealthy among us.

More than becoming rich, we want the material goods that accompany getting and keeping money. Celebrities come into our living rooms via infomercials and twenty-four-hour-a-day home shopping channels, trying to convince us that we can make our lives easier, our bodies thinner, and our health better by buying their products. We see bumper stickers that read "He who has the most toys when he dies, wins." Pop star Madonna celebrates being a "Material Girl," and truly, we are a materialistic society.

How can we not be? We're told we can buy now and pay later. Easy credit, low interest, no interest. We can get credit cards easily and quickly, whether we have the income to pay them off or not. Daily, our mailboxes overflow with a newly delivered stack of catalogues and flyers that encourage us to spend our money on products we probably didn't even know existed until we saw them in catalogues! The media bombard us with carefully crafted advertisements designed to convince us to buy items we really don't need. We wear designer clothes and even eat designer foods, whether we can afford to or not.

We're not saying that wanting a better life and having nice things are wrong. What we are suggesting is that we look closely at our motivations about money, and that we realize the importance of maintaining a balance between what we want and what we need. This balance, however, is increasingly difficult to achieve. Distractions and temptations abound. Following are some of the ways money addictions can manifest themselves in our lives.

## Compulsive or Emotional Spending

Compulsive or emotional spending is one of the ways we get out of balance. Men and women both overspend and shop compulsively; they just do it differently. Generally, men are more likely to overspend on computers and cars, while women choose clothes, cosmetics, and items for the home. Compulsive spenders shop out of emotional rather than actual need. They shop to fill gaps in their soul rather than gaps in their closet. Shopping is used for comfort and to feel more alive. It also can be used as a means of venting emotions that feel too threatening for direct expression. Frequently, the shopper's purchases sit in the closet, unnoticed and untouched, a silent witness to needs that cannot be met by material goods. The purchase, of course, wasn't the point. Listen to what these women have to say about the subject:

> "When I am depressed, I do tend to spend more money."
> "I have the belief that money can buy happiness or at least it can numb out the pain, anger, and loneliness for awhile. I shop or purchase things for comfort. Like any other addiction, it only brings temporary relief to a deeper problem."

Compulsive spending may come from simply not knowing how to deal with money of our own. In the past, women usually did not have direct spending power because we were not the primary wage earners. Our money came from our husbands or fathers. It may have been freely given, doled out as an allowance, or withheld as control. Regardless, it was not ours. The stereotype of the farmer's wife putting aside some of the egg money so she had "a little of her own" has its basis in fact. In our workshops, we find that a majority of married women admit to having a secret fund that they do not plan to tell their partners about. These women recognize the way money can give security, balance a relationship, and even out the power.

Compulsive spending can also be used for an unconscious purpose. Marriage and family therapists have long been aware of the way money is used to express deeper problems within the family relationship. A shopping spree with a charge card is a quick and easy way to get back at an unresponsive spouse or parent. The college student away from home for the first time who overspends with her parents' charge card gets their attention in a way her grades do not. The wife who is unhappy in her marriage and deals with her anger and hurt by buying new clothes gets revenge in a subtle but clear way. Frequently in a relationship in which there is unacknowledged anger, hurt, or fear, overspending is a way the passive family member expresses with her actions what she cannot say with her words. In the workplace, these unresolved feelings can manifest themselves in the overuse of an expense account. That certainly gets the boss's attention!

In her classic book, *The Dance of Anger*, Harriet Goldhor Lerner discusses the difficulties women have dealing with the outright expression of anger, and points out that our society sees it as an unacceptable emotion for women.[1] This being the case, compulsive spending is sometimes a substitute for honest, direct expression of anger. We might label this behavior as a semi-effective survival skill, since it is a way to express emotions when we believe other avenues are closed.

Compulsive spending is not a growth-producing choice even if it hasn't progressed to the point where it gets the spender in deep financial trouble. This unhealthy behavior pattern attempts to fill an emotional void with material goods or express feelings that don't seem to be safe to deal with openly. Further, it keeps the spender unbalanced and diverts the focus of energy away from health and healing. Understanding this pattern of behavior can help us get off the money treadmill.

Look back at your money genogram and review the spending patterns of the women in your family. We sometimes repeat these patterns unconsciously even though they serve no useful purpose now. Do you see any patterns in your family?

The following exercise is designed to help you identify compulsive/emotional shopping. We urge all our readers to try this exercise.

Take a few minutes to sit quietly and be alone with your thoughts. Take some deep, relaxing breaths and allow your mind to drift back to your last shopping trip. Where did you go? What was your motivation for shopping? What emotions did you bring with you on this trip? How much planning went into your purchases? What did you buy? How did you pay for your purchases? Did you go into debt to make the purchases? If so, how did you plan to pay off your charge cards? How did you feel after the shopping trip? Was this a typical shopping excursion or was it different from your usual experience?

You may wish to repeat this exercise with several past shopping trips, asking yourself the same questions. Do you see any patterns? Make notes about what you have learned from this exercise. Then complete the following sentence:

As a result of this exercise, I now realize that I _____

_____.

Answering the following questions can also help you identify your behaviors:

Do you frequently fight with a significant person in your life over money? How do the fights usually go? How are they resolved?

How many credit cards do you have? Do you frequently use one credit card to pay off another? What is your average yearly interest charge on each of your credit cards? Has your credit card ever been repossessed by the lending agency?

Do you see charges on your charge bill that come as a surprise because you have forgotten about purchases you made?

Do you tend to use shopping to reward yourself?

Do you buy things knowing that in a few days you will return them?

If you have identified any compulsive/emotional shopping patterns, write them down and complete the following sentence:

As a result of this exercise, I now realize that I _____

_____.

Now, breathe, relax, and envision an ideal shopping experience excursion, one that is free of ulterior motivations. Allow this experience to fully saturate your being, knowing as you do this that you are paving the way for a healthier relationship with money.

We need to be careful to remain nonjudgmental when we look at any compulsive spending patterns we may have. We are looking for information to facilitate change, not to use to beat ourselves up. Remember, those of us who are compulsive spenders found ourselves in situations where we felt we had no power and thus didn't dare express our emotions. It may have become habitual behavior that we slip into when we feel scared, hurt or angry. Now, there are other choices we can make that reflect our personal development and are more in line with who we are today.

If you believe you are a compulsive shopper and need help, know that there are several organizations available to help you. Debtors Anonymous, based on the twelve-step principles of Alcoholics Anonymous, is one of the most common. Most communities also have consumer debtors' organizations to help you get control of your spending. You can find these or other self-help organizations in the phone book or by calling your local social service information and referral center for a recommendation.

## Pamela's Story

Pamela explained that in her family, affection meant another dress or new shoes. She and her brother both had so many clothes and toys that a lot of their friends envied them. She remembered fondly how close she felt to her mother—when they were shopping. At other times, both parents were emotionally distant, preoccupied with their own careers. Only after some extended therapy as an adult did Pamela realize she had been using material things to substitute for emotions. She found herself in a relationship where she was frequently showered with gifts. At first, she enjoyed these attentions. But she soon realized that she felt hollow and unfulfilled, a familiar, distressing feeling. In therapy she learned that she was repeating her family pattern in the relationship. She had the courage to break it off only to find herself facing another dilemma. She began spending compulsively, again to fill in the emptiness she felt. After her therapist helped her understand what she was doing, she resolved to make some changes. She told us how she broke her compulsive spending habits.

First, I destroyed all but one of my credit cards. Then I put the one remaining card in a bowl of water and stuck it in the freezer. Now when I'm tempted to splurge, I have to wait for the water to melt. That takes hours! By that time the urge has passed and I've identified the emotional motivation behind the desire. And I've promised myself I won't use the microwave to thaw it faster. After all, I want to be a success at this. I'm also in a much healthier relationship now. One of my first rules was no gifts except for certain special occasions.

## Guilty Spending

Guilty spending is the flip side of compulsive spending. This attitude frequently comes from childhood messages that there is never enough. Now, as an adult, no joy comes from buying something we want. Rooted in a mentality of scarcity, this belief keeps us constantly in fear. Guilt is a word used over and over by the women in our workshops. Again, women's voices:

> "I have guilt in spending, having to self-justify before spending, seeking approval and reward for saving."
>
> "I rarely buy some big item unless it's on sale. I rarely get rid of something until it's absolutely used up. I was in my mid-twenties before I bought bread that wasn't day old."
>
> "I document almost all the money that comes in and goes out of the house. I also make almost all of the financial decisions. I feel stressed if I go more than one week without documenting expenses and updating our financial forecast."
>
> "I feel guilty when I spend it."
>
> "I have a very unflashy life and am probably even a bit eccentric in *not* spending money."

What did you learn about this message when you went through Chapter 2, Exploring Your Money Messages? The strength of your family messages can determine the strength of this pattern of addiction.

The guilty spending pattern is unhealthy because it is not based on current reality, but rather on past fears and old messages. Many women constantly struggle with spending the smallest amounts of money and worry that there is not enough. Their belief in the "not enough theory" limits them emotionally, keeps them controlled by fear, and doesn't allow them to gain the confidence that they can deal with money in a healthy manner. Worry and guilt, especially about money, can be seductive. Engaging in these behaviors feels like a lot of activity—look how much time we can spend doing it! The risk is that we'll mistake emotion for activity. We frequently confuse the amount of time spent worrying and feeling guilty with the actual resolving of our issues.

A variation on the guilty spending pattern is our willingness to buy for everyone in the world except ourselves. It seems that if we are not worrying about having enough money, we are giving it away to show what good people we are. Frequently women tell us about shopping for their husbands or children and being unable to spend on themselves. How often have you seen women dressed in obviously well-worn clothes who are accompanied by their children in designer jeans and wearing expensive shoes? Two of our respondents summed up this attitude: "I'm more comfortable giving than receiving. I often put others ahead of myself," Shirley, a business owner, said. "I have always put my family's needs first," a nurse told us.

Putting others first financially isn't restricted to women in comfortable lifestyles. A young woman living in poverty and receiving food stamps told us, "It's only the second week of the month and my food stamps are gone already. My friend has kids and I figured she needed them more than I did so I gave most of mine to her."

We come by this give-it-away belief in a variety of ways. Susan told us that she got contradictory messages growing up: "Money is the root of all evil, but money is God's. Give Him 10 percent of all you make and you will be continually blessed with more of this money. If you are good, God will meet your needs."

An old fairy tale, *Shower of Gold*, tells of a little girl who gave away all she had until she stood naked and cold. A shower of gold coins rained down from the heavens, rewarding her for her selflessness. The message to women is clear: We have to give it all away to be worthy. We expand on this concept in Chapter 9.

We are definitely not recommending that women stop giving. As women, our history, instincts, and socialization lead us to be concerned about the well-being of others. Feminine nurturing is a special quality—one that we don't want to negate or to lose. Again, however, the issue is one of balance. If we are giving at our own expense, we fall into the giving-to-get trap. We give because we want people to think well of us, because we don't believe we are worthy of nice things, because we are seeking self-esteem from being overconcerned with others. This approach is destined to fail because it is based on a faulty assumption that goes something like, "I only have value when I give to others," or "I only count when I am putting myself last." In the end we are depleted because we have neglected to nurture ourselves.

In counseling sessions with women, Kay frequently uses the analogy of an airplane leaving the ground to explain this notion. When the flight attendants give safety instructions, they always tell us what will happen if cabin pressure falls. Oxygen masks will automatically drop, we are told, and people flying with infants or small children should adjust their own masks *first* before attempting to help those who are dependent on them. This is sound reasoning, for if the helper passes out from oxygen deprivation, who then will care for the child? Without self-care, we are of no use to anyone else. Our task is to affirm our intrinsic self-worth and recognize that giving and getting, like other things in life, must be kept in balance. The bottom line is, be sure your own oxygen mask is firmly secured before you attempt to help anyone else.

Try the following exercise to check out your giving/getting ratio. Read through the directions before starting.

Take a deep breath and close your eyes. Visualize an old-fashioned balance scale. It has baskets or bins hanging on each side of a center point, and an item placed in one basket will affect the balance of the other side. Your scale can be any color and size you chose, as ornate or simple as you wish.

Label one side of the center point **What I Give** and the other, **What I Get**. See one side fill up with the aspect of your life that has to do with giving. You might visualize what you do for your family, or perhaps your volunteer work. Then watch the other side fill up with the aspect of your life having to do with getting. Perhaps you'll see your friendships or love relationship here. Pick those aspects most meaningful to your life. And pay attention to any guilt feelings that may arise as you balance the scales. Remind yourself of the oxygen mask. Let go of the guilt then replace it with calm acceptance.

Look carefully at your vision, without censoring or judging. Are the sides in balance or is one side heavier than the other? If so, which one? What meaning does this information have for you in terms of your giving/getting balance? Are there changes you need to make to bring more balance to your life? If so, what?

Write your vision here:

Let these mental pictures help you as you move toward a healthier relationship with money.

## *Amy's Story*

When we first met Amy, she was a participant in one of our early workshops. During our discussion of money issues around guilty spending and giving rather than receiving, she became somewhat agitated. After several women discussed their habits in this area and demonstrated a desire to change, Amy finally spoke up. She was very upset with the "selfish" tone of the discussion and said that she wouldn't feel right putting herself first. As a bank teller for many years, Amy told us about how helpful she had been to all the management trainees. She was proud of the fact that several were now branch managers or held even higher positions. When one of the participants asked her what reward she received for teaching them, she replied that she didn't need a reward. When another woman asked her why she wasn't a branch manager, Amy stated that she never thought about it.

The group continued to discuss guilty spending issues but we noticed that Amy had become preoccupied. We heard nothing from her until she appeared at another money workshop the following year. When the subject of the giving/getting ratio came up, Amy burst forth with her insights.

I thought you two were crazy when we talked about this before. "Selfish" was the word that kept running through my mind. When I went back to work I began to count up how many people I had helped to advance their careers. And there I was, stuck in the same place for eight years. Not one of them helped me! When I looked at my life, I discovered that I had a lot of friends who depended on me for everything from rides to the doctor to a sympathetic ear. It struck me that things were really out of balance.

Then an amazing thing happened—I broke my leg skiing and had to ask others for help. And you know what? Most of those people I had been helping were too busy. I heard those women in the first workshop asking me about my attitudes about helping others and I finally heard the message. I was letting myself be used and abused. As my body was healing, I began making lists of changes I wanted to make in my life. I vowed that the next time an opening came up at work that would be a promotion, I was going for it. And I'm here to tell you I got it! I also cleaned house regarding my friends. This was hard, but now I'm making new friendships that are more balanced with give and take. And I now understand that my value as a person doesn't come from what I give or what I get, it comes from me just being me.

Now that I've got this balance thing straight, I'm here to look at the rest of my money issues.

## Avoiding Intimacy

Another aspect of the addictive money treadmill can lead to the avoidance of intimacy. When we become addicted to money, it takes the place of emotions, replacing people as our primary focus and thus becoming more important than relationships. There is no room in our lives for anything but accumulating and holding onto our drug of choice. While this pattern is more commonly seen in men (probably because, traditionally, they have been the ones with the most money), we know that women are not immune. We all have heard tales of the recluse who died alone and friendless and yet was found with millions of dollars in her mattress or savings account. We are familiar with the mother who was so preoccupied with acquiring wealth that she gave her children's activities a lower priority than her business meetings. We know about women who choose financial success over relationships. This is the stuff that makes material for the movie of the week or romance novels.

Such women are both fascinating and repellent at the same time because they illustrate our own love–hate relationship with wealth. We fear that our quest for money will get out of control. Remember the story of King Midas who wished that everything he touched could be turned into gold? He had a wonderful time with his newly found power until his young daughter ran into his arms and was turned into a frozen statue of gold. This cautionary tale illustrates the dangers of a misplaced focus on wealth. As King Midas learned his lesson, so must we. A misplaced focus on money will be punished.

The preoccupation with getting and hanging onto money keeps

us constantly in motion. It sets us up to become workaholics. We seek and never find enough. Indeed, the process of seeking becomes an end in itself, and calls for an energy expenditure that leaves little room for anything else. For those of us who are afraid of intimacy, this seeking can serve as a convenient excuse. "When I become financially secure, I'll be ready to have a relationship," we tell ourselves, but that security keeps moving beyond our reach as we move toward new goals. Thus we are never "ready" for a relationship. According to one woman, "Achievements have always led to income and [thus] to greater aspirations." The organizations we work for may love our productivity, but who loves us as an individual?

We also fear that someone will not love us for ourselves but rather for our money. A Henry James story, *Washington Square*, tells such a tale of a young woman deceived by a lover wanting only her money. It's a common theme on television and in novels. Another woman told us, "I have a hard time trusting that anyone could possibly just want me for me and not my money. It takes a long time to trust that someone would love me if I didn't have it. I don't *ever* want to think I'm buying love."

We are caught in the search for intimacy, fearing it and wanting it at the same time. We substitute money for intimacy and feel we have made a bad bargain, yet we aren't sure how to do anything else. Further, as with other addictions, addiction to money leads to a feeling of worthlessness, a poverty of the spirit, and lowered self-esteem, regardless of our level of productivity. Basing our self-worth and self-esteem on money is a false goal. Many of the women responding to our survey were clear that money doesn't guarantee happiness and emotional well-being. For example:

"Money is not happiness but it can enhance happiness."
"Money isn't everything. Even if I had all the money in the world
I would still have problems—maybe more if I had money."

How do we know if a focus on money is keeping us from intimacy? Return to the questionnaire at the end of Chapter 1. Refer specifically to questions 3 and 6. What do you see in your answers regarding your relationship to money (question 3) and money and relationships (question 6)? Do you see any answers you gave that could demonstrate an attempt to substitute money for intimacy? Now take another look at your money family tree. Do you see any patterns here that need attention? Is there anything you need to add to either of these sections now that you know more about money as an addiction? Write your thoughts here:

_____

_____

_____

Understanding how money can be used to avoid intimacy can result in startling changes in your relationship with money as well as with other people.

## Harriet's Story

Harriet originally came into therapy for stress management. Her high blood pressure was not adequately responding to medication, so her doctor pushed her to get additional help. She was a successful hospital administrator who had a reputation for being a hard-nosed manager. She demanded and got increased productivity while trimming budgets. And she virtually lived at her workplace. Seven days a week, she divided her time among attending meetings, working at her computer, walking the hospital corridors, and traveling to conferences. She was so devoted to her work that she didn't even own a houseplant. "I don't have time to water it," she explained. While Harriet initially wanted some quick techniques for lowering her stress, she soon realized that her physical symptoms had a deeper cause that needed to be addressed.

> When I was in college, my fiancé was killed in an automobile accident. It was the first time in my life I ever had to deal with the death of someone close to me. I was devastated. I threw myself into my schoolwork rather than deal with my pain. When I graduated, I kept up that same workaholic lifestyle. I've accomplished a lot because of it and I've gotten a lot of rewards. But my life is now killing me. I realize that my addiction to work has enabled me to avoid an intimate relationship where I might get hurt again.

Harriet then began her long journey of allowing herself to feel her grief while slowly extracting herself from her intensive level of work. During this process she decided to take a job in a small hospital where she could work a more normal schedule while developing long-buried interests that would balance her life.

## Getting Off the Treadmill

Compulsive spending, guilty spending, giving it all away, and using money to block intimacy are variations on a theme of money addiction. These aspects of the money treadmill give the illusion of much movement, but really get us nowhere. Our task is to recognize these as outdated behaviors and get off the treadmill. How do we do that? Use the following list to help distinguish a healthy relationship with money from an unhealthy one. Check the choice that fits you best.

☐ The more money I have, the more secure I feel.
☐ To me, money is merely a means to an end. My sense of security comes from within myself.

- [ ] I either think about money all the time or I ignore it all together.
- [ ] My thoughts about money are neither all-consuming nor nonexistent.

- [ ] The more things I have, the more I want. So I work to earn money to buy the things I want.
- [ ] While I enjoy having material things, they are not the most important aspects of my life.

- [ ] The more money I have, the more valuable I am as a person.
- [ ] How much money I have or don't have has nothing to do with how I feel about myself.

- [ ] There is only so much money available to each of us, so I need to hang on to what I have.
- [ ] There's always a flow of money in my life, so I can take risks because I know I will be all right in the long run.

- [ ] To feel good about myself, I buy clothes that I really can't afford, or pick up the check in an expensive restaurant to impress my friends.
- [ ] I am comfortable living within my means, even when I don't have the amount of money some of my friends do.

- [ ] It's nobody's business how much money I make, so no one in my life knows how much I earn.
- [ ] When it's appropriate, I am comfortable discussing money with people in my life.

- [ ] The people close to me know that if they make me mad, I'll cut them out of my will.
- [ ] I take care of myself first and I enjoy charitable giving. I make certain those I love are provided for in my will (or living trust).

- [ ] I worry a lot about money. I often get overwhelmed about money issues.

- [ ] Money is just another tool I have to help me live the way I want to.

- [ ] I have a driving need to obtain as much money as I can. I have become a workaholic in this quest.
- [ ] I control my money. It doesn't control me.

- [ ] I'm just not good at making money decisions. I'm afraid of making the wrong decision, and I experience a lot of stress around money. I haven't made much progress in my relationship with money during my adult life.
- [ ] The money in my life, like my other relationships, supports me in fulfilling who I am. It enables me to live my life as I choose.

Quite obviously, the second statement in each pair describes a much healthier relationship with money than the first assertion. You may find yourself clearly described in one or the other statement. Or you may see yourself somewhere between the two beliefs. Regardless of where you find yourself, by focusing on the healthy relationship statements, you can begin developing a new vision of how you want to relate with money.

*Chapter Seven*

# Burying Your Head in the Coins

We're all familiar with the folk legend of the ostrich that buries her head in the sand when she encounters a frightening situation. Lulled into an illusion of safety because she can't see what's happening around her, the big bird supposedly feels comforted. Alas, poor ostrich. What she forgets is that while one-tenth of her is covered, nine-tenths of her is exposed to the world and all its dangers. The ostrich has forgotten that old survival maxim, "Always cover your behind."

Now we know that an ostrich really doesn't bury her head in the sand. In truth, she doesn't need to. Weighing in at upward of 300 pounds and achieving a height of more than eight feet, she is the largest bird alive today, and can probably handle danger just fine. Nevertheless, putting one's head in the sand as a technique for avoiding danger is an image that still lingers in our popular fiction.

Our experience working with women (as well as coming to grips with our own financial foibles!) suggests that women employ a similar defense strategy when it comes to money. The authors have termed this practice "burying our heads in a pile of coins." In other words, even though we are surrounded by money and need it to survive, at the same time we don't want to know about it. Some of us go even further and sabotage ourselves in our dealings with the financial future. "Let the rest of the world come and go," we say. "We'll just stay right here with our heads in the coins." But, like the ostrich, we tend to forget that more of us is exposed than is covered! Our safety is only an illusion, but because we concentrate so hard on staying hidden, we lose sight of the fact that we really *can* cope with our finances.

Do we really find comfort and safety in this lack of knowledge about how to handle money? Are we really so disinterested in learning about it? It would seem so. Young women in a 1992 UCLA study were found to fear money more, learn about handling it later, work less, and receive more financial support from parents than their male counterparts.[1]

And difficulty dealing with money is not limited to unsophisticated college-age women. A recent survey of investors showed that only 11 percent of the women polled could be rated as very knowledgeable about their own investments.[2] Another survey tells us that 62 percent of women said they did not know what a mutual fund was, while another 89 percent said they did not track the Dow Jones Averages. The fact that only 25 percent of the men could be rated as very knowledgeable is small comfort.[3] While some other surveys are more optimistic about investors' knowledge, that fact remains that we do have a long way to go.[4]

Many of us have gone too long with our heads in the coins, waiting and hoping that someone else will take responsibility for our money life, or that we can make our problems go away by ignoring them. Realistically, this is not going to happen, and on some level we know it. We have seen women suddenly plunged into poverty as widows or divorcees. We constantly read articles telling us that women don't plan adequately for their old age and thus face the probability of financial hard times. The message is clear: As much as we might wish them to, our money issues just won't go away. So, if financial ignorance is no longer bliss, we must face the fact that the time to become our own financial experts has arrived.

This doesn't mean we have to do every last piece of our financial work ourselves. (See Chapter 17 for a discussion of various possibilities.) It does mean that we must take a more active role in managing this aspect of life. We have a variety of choices as to how we do it, but do it we must! It is critical that we know what's going on with *our* money and participate in its management. We must pull our heads out of the coins and deal with our finances in a rational and clearheaded way.

What helps us maintain the fantasy that ignoring a vital piece of our survival and well being is a desirable coping strategy? How did we end up with our heads buried in the coins? Let's look at some of the paths we may have taken to get to this point. Then, in Chapter 8, we'll discuss what we can do to change these behaviors. Clearly it is time to take our head out of the coins and look around us. In so doing, we may find that life on the financial frontier is much less scary than we imagined.

## Messages From Family and Society

Many of us were taught either directly or indirectly by our families that it was OK *not* to be knowledgeable about money. Perhaps we saw our mothers and grandmothers turn financial planning over to the men in the family, or at least go along with the pretense of doing so. While women handled the small day-to-day finances, men made the "important" decisions. We might have grown up watching our brothers take more responsible and higher paying jobs, or heard that limited family resources needed to be spent educating male instead of female siblings. Possibly we observed money being used as a means of control over family members. We may even have seen beyond-the-grave control as family members were cut out of a relative's will for perceived misbehaviors or rewarded for good ones.

As we learned in Chapter 2, most family messages are powerful and have a lasting effect on us. Family *money* messages are doubly problematic. Not only are they filled with strength and emotion, but they are also frequently implied rather than spoken. These implied, or indirect, messages are the most difficult for us as adults to articulate and contest. Their subtle shaping gives them staying power, and they are ingrained in our unconscious belief system.

Society's messages also helped shape our belief system. Most of us were told in many ways that we didn't need to bother about money. Our images in the media were usually of women who found Mr. Right, the caretaker/prince they sought. Movies and novels showed us how to wait for him to come along (patiently and virtuously) and what to do while we waited (keep ourselves thin and beautiful). Further, we were told that it was unladylike to deal with finances. Money was dirty—as in "filthy rich," "filthy lucre," or "stinking rich."

Betty Lehan Harragan, a guru of corporate gamesmanship, observed, "Women have been so brainwashed by the destructive female culture that taught them to associate money with sin, evil, and everything crude, vulgar, filthy, ill-bred, crass, dirty, unladylike, unfeminine, gauche, and obscene that they cannot separate money from uteri." She goes on to say, "The roots of this psychic crippling go so deep into the subjugation of women that it would take an entire book to untangle the subconscious fears and incredible fantasies that the simple noun 'money' evokes in most women."[5] In other words, the messages women have received regarding how best to interact with money have given most of us permission to remain unaware and uninformed.

In the past, we have had very few role models for dealing with finances on our own. The women in our books, films, and television shows happily turned their financial hopes and dreams over to the men in their lives. Are you aware of messages that have been particularly strong in your life? While the picture is improving, many of us still carry the residuals of old programming. We have already discussed the perils and pitfalls inherent in this behavior choice in Chapter 3.

## Attitudes of Financial Institutions

Another factor contributing to the head-in-the-coins phenomenon is the fact that, until recently, financial institutions and brokers have largely ignored women. We weren't considered a financial force to be reckoned with, and thus the message that we shouldn't and couldn't deal with our own money was reinforced. Studies in both 1993 and 1994 by *Money* magazine documented how brokers failed to take women investors seriously. Women weren't pursued by brokers as potential clients and when brokers did work with women, they gave them less help than male customers. Women got less time with their brokers than did men, were given fewer choices among investments, and were steered away from or not even told about investment possibilities involving higher risk. In several instances, brokers asked to speak to the woman's spouse on the phone or she was told to bring him in to the office.[6] None of the male investors was asked to bring his wife in, a fact that probably does not surprise any woman.

Not only are we treated worse than men were by brokers, but we also seem to lack the sophistication to know that we are being mistreated. In the survey, women rated their satisfaction with their brokers more highly than men did. But when both men and women were asked whether service or rate of return played the more important role in their choice of a financial institution, men said rate of return; women chose service. Says Karen Altfest, a certified financial planner, "Women are often less experienced investors. They don't necessarily know when a broker is really being helpful or not."[7]

This orientation leaves us in a vulnerable position. Women expect less from our brokers and financial institutions and we get it. Has this ever happened to you?

## Our Saving Patterns and Retirement

Women and men save differently. Men save for their retirements, while women are more likely to save with others' well-being in mind.

95

Women save for their children's education, a nicer house in a better neighborhood, more comfortable home furnishings, family vacations. Moreover, women tend to start saving for retirement later in life because we tend to take care of everyone else first or because we interrupt our careers while we raise families.

A psychotherapist admitted to us, "I'm struggling now, am in debt and am fearful about what the circumstances will be when I retire." Smart woman! She has good reason to be worried. You may share her concerns. Many women have gotten themselves into a bind over money because they have been unwilling to look at the harsher realities, such as the following:

- Women spend fewer years working than men do and thus accumulate less. Because we are out of the workforce raising children or caring for parents or other family members, we have less in our savings and pension funds when retirement rolls around. Some of us may have taken a lower paying job while we put a spouse through college, thus postponing our career development and lowering our overall retirement resources.[8]
- Women earn less overall—71 percent of men's wages—and are more likely to work part-time than men. According to the Bureau of Labor Statistics, six out of every ten minimum-wage workers is female. Sixty-one percent of all part-time workers are women, and only 15 percent of part-time workers are covered by a pension plan.[9]
- Women are 50 percent less likely than men to have an employer-provided pension. When women do receive a pension, it will pay less than men receive—an average of fifty percent less![10]
- A woman's Social Security benefits at retirement will probably be less than those received by men. Since Social Security payments are based on the average salaries over the working

years, fewer years in the workforce and lower pay while working will drag down the woman's average.[11]

- A woman's marital status has a large impact on her financial security at retirement. A widow is four times more likely to live in poverty than a married woman, while a divorced or single woman is five times more likely to be at poverty level.[12]

These figures paint a bleak picture. You may even know women who are in these very situations, perhaps including yourself. We need to see these realities as our call to action. Since the prince isn't coming and we aren't likely to win the lottery, we need to change this outlook for ourselves. The good news is that we can do just that by ridding ourselves of unhealthy money messages and choosing to define money on our terms according to how we want it to serve us.

## Our Own Attitudes

To celebrate its twenty-fifth anniversary, *New Woman* magazine produced a special issue. One of the features listed "The 25 Most Important Moments in a Woman's Life," which, according to editor-in-chief Betsy Carter, "reflected the spectrum of a woman's life."[13] Only *one* of the twenty-five important life moments had anything to do with money, and even then it was an indirect reference. The main thrust of the article had to do with career passages, not taking charge of one's financial life.

We believe this feature illustrates a difference in how men and women think about money. Most of us would probably not place an event having to do with money on our personal list of the twenty-five most important moments of our lives. It isn't that money has no importance to us; we simply don't think about it. We've been taught that it is not appropriate for us as women to do so. Yet men have a quite different outlook.

A survey on self-esteem in a popular woman's magazine demonstrates a key male-female difference in thinking about what role money plays in our lives.[14] When respondents were asked to prioritize the essential elements of self-esteem, men replied that the number one key to their self-esteem was to earn $30,000 or more per year. Women listed satisfaction with body and looks as their first choice. The women surveyed did list having paid work in second place, but without specifying a dollar amount.

Interestingly, not only do men put money in first place on their determinants of self-esteem scale, but they also seem to know exactly how much it would take for them to feel good about themselves—$30,000 or more per year! Women don't have this same certainty when it comes to money issues. Money doesn't figure into our definition of Self in quite the same way, and thus we tend not to think about it as clearly or as often as men do. This doesn't mean women can't think about money, it simply means we don't. As one woman in our survey said, "I avoid it. I want my husband to earn it. I feel incapable of making it."

Men are more confident about money than women. Indeed, they are four times more likely than women to perceive themselves as experts when it comes to finances.[15] Reflecting this lack of confidence, women tend to worry more about money. A 1996 *Money* magazine survey found that 29 percent of women say they worry about money very often, while only 17 percent of men reported doing so.[16] We worry more *and* we worry differently. Men are concerned about losing face or not having enough money to pay the mortgage.[17] Women are more likely to fret about day-to-day issues, as in making it from paycheck to paycheck. Even well-paid women earning between $35,000 and $75,000 per year report concern over living close to the financial edge.[18]

If we are struggling and worried about making ends meet, it makes sense that we would be more concerned with our money's safety than its ability to grow. According the *Kiplinger's Personal Fi-*

*nance* magazine, a woman with $10,000 to invest is more likely to put it in a bank than to invest in a more risky venture.[19] The problem with being *this* safe is that it hinders both our investment capability and our potential for increased financial resources. The experts tells us that in order to live a decent lifestyle on retirement, we need to invest in something other than passbook savings or low-risk certificates of deposit. Yet because of our lack of confidence in our financial abilities, coupled with our general money worries, women tend to be much more conservative when it comes to investing.

## Our Sabotaging Behaviors

There are several ways women sabotage themselves when it comes to financial dealings. As we look at them, consider if any are active in your life.

One reason we allow ourselves to ignore taking control of our finances is fear. Stories abound in magazines and newspapers detailing the problems we will face in our declining years. The common thread running through many of these articles is that we don't save and even if we do, we will still have poverty-stricken lives in our retirement. These stories are indeed discomforting. They touch on some of our deepest fears about being unable to care for ourselves, becoming welfare dependent, or worse yet, being bag ladies. "The prevalence of bag-lady fears, particularly among professional women who are beyond economic dependence on a man, is really quite astonishing," writes *Passages* author Gail Sheehy.[20] As we mention in Chapter 5, the bag-lady fear is shared by a majority of the women we work with on money issues. It may occupy the top spot on your list of worries as well. If it does, now you know you are not alone in your concern.

Some women are so frightened by the dire predictions they read about retirement perils that they find themselves paralyzed by fear.

How did you react as you read over the figures earlier in this chapter? Fear can become a reason to sabotage self-care behavior. "It's really hard for me and it won't make any difference anyway" goes the reasoning. With this rationale firmly planted in our consciousness, we feel justified in continuing to ignore dealing with money. We allow ourselves to become overwhelmed with fear, then we sabotage ourselves with inaction.

A second way we undermine ourselves is to be sure we have no money left at the end of the month. Many women in our workshops confessed to setting themselves up to have little or no money to invest for the future. One woman told us that she experienced a feeling of relief when she was out of money by the end of the month because then she knew she didn't have to deal with investing or saving it! It was just gone, and for her that was comforting. Another woman said, "When I have money I seem to be in a frenzy until it is gone." This mind-set often motivates impulsive spending and ensures there will be no money to invest.

A closely related way of maintaining head-in-the-coins behavior is to ignore the daily aspects of money management. For example, one woman stated, "I am lucky to have a husband I can trust to take care of me. I let him figure out the household bills." Another woman we know can't deal with the stress of bill paying and copes by just tossing all incoming bills into a desk drawer. She leaves them untouched until the tension of knowing the bills are sitting there outweighs the fear of having to pay them. It may take several months before she builds up incentive to deal with them. Meanwhile, overdue charges accrue and her credit rating suffers. This is an extreme example of head-in-the-coins behavior, but most of us have experienced some variation on this theme. Is this fear operating in your life?

Yet another issue for women is having unclear goals when it comes to dealing with our financial life. Merrill Lynch's Seventh Annual Retirement and Financial Planning Survey revealed that 41 percent of women as opposed to 28 percent of men say they have not "clearly identified long-term financial goals."[21] Many of us just don't know how to plan for the future. We haven't had to until now, so it is a skill we have yet to develop. For others of us, failure to plan is one more way of ignoring our money issues. We need to see that this head-in-the-coins behavior won't keep us from danger; it is merely an illusion of safety. Sooner or later we need to face down our financial demons and cope with the future.

The purpose these various avoidance behaviors serve is to keep us from having to deal with that burdensome issue—money. If we don't have any, we are freed from taking charge of our lives, spared from making scary decisions and taking risks. If we are frozen in fear and can't act, we have yet another reason for not taking action. If we don't have a plan, we can be excused from moving in a positive direction, or any direction at all.

We may experience short-term relief with these behaviors, but in the long run we are doomed to add stress and worry to our lives. Avoidance is a mistaken strategy that leads us in the wrong direction. As with other fear-based behaviors, self-sabotage about our money issues lays the groundwork for frustration, discomfort, and dread.

Take a few minutes before you read further to list any fear-based behaviors currently operating in your life.

My fear-based behaviors are:

_____

_____

_____

"Money is such a head trip," said Marilyn, an independent sales distributor. She is right. Exactly how much of a head trip is demonstrated by how we allow old messages from family and society to control our lives and how we self-sabotage so that we fail to take care of our future.

Armed with this awareness, we're ready to look at what we can do about pulling our heads out of the coins.

## *Sylvia's Story*

Sylvia is fairly typical of many of the women who have come to our workshops. She has her career, yet has not really planned financially for her retirement. With her fortieth birthday came the realization that she needed to take some action regarding her finances.

> I didn't think turning forty would mean that much. But it hit me harder that I thought it would. Maybe it's because I have my married sisters and I realized that I'll probably have to take care of myself. Maybe I just accepted that retirement really would actually happen to me.
>
> I had gathered a bunch of information about investing. I even took an investment class at the community college. But for some reason, I just couldn't bring myself to do anything with my new knowledge. I just kept putting off making a decision about investments. To tell the truth, I was frightened of making a mistake and losing some money. Eventually I realized how much money I was losing by keeping it all in the bank. Still, I was frozen.
>
> Then a friend suggested that I talk to her financial planner. What an eye opener! She made planning my financial future seem like something I could really do. I finally came to terms with the fact that if I don't make my own financial decisions, nobody's going to do it for me. At the same time I became aware that I must have some negative beliefs that are keeping me from moving forward. So I'm looking at

my money messages and at the same time I've joined an investment club. That way, I have a real incentive to work through any belief that's holding me back. And being part of the club means I'm taking responsibility about money. As I do that, I have to come to terms with any ways I might sabotage myself. I've gotten to the place where I actually look forward to discovering any negative beliefs I still have because I know that as I clear them out, I move closer to being financially secure.

*Chapter Eight*

# $\mathscr{P}$ulling Your Head Out of the Coins

In Chapter 7, we cite a number of studies and surveys showing women's generally unhappy relationship with money. What these facts neglect to point out is that we can change our circumstances. We are in charge of how we want to relate to money and even how we want to define it. Shirley, a business owner, observed: "Women must be deprogrammed regarding perceptions of money and power. Men control and manipulate because women in general defer their God-given rights. Women must educate themselves concerning finances—how to get money and how to invest it wisely."

We couldn't agree more. Let's explore some ways to deprogram ourselves and pull our heads out of the coins.

## Rewriting Your Messages

Awareness of old messages about women's role regarding money gives us the power to rewrite them. The old messages said that women can't, don't, and shouldn't deal with money issues. It's time to erase these old messages and embrace new ones. Try this exercise:

Have ready a large pad of paper and a pen, pencil, or crayon. On your paper draw a vertical line dividing the page into two sides. Write **Old Messages** on the left side and then write **New Messages** on the right side. Now sit comfortably in your chair. Take in a few easy breaths and let them out gently. Allow yourself to get in touch with any old family and societal messages you believe are still affecting your life today. Writing down your first thoughts as quickly as you can, jot down as many old messages as come to mind. Don't filter. When you feel completed, stop and take a few deep breaths.

Now read what you have written. Tell yourself, "That was then, this is now. I am ready to move on." Using the second side of the page, counter each message with an updated one that fits who you are today. For example, if you wrote as an old message, "Women in our family turn money matters over to men," your new message might be, "I am capable of handling my own money concerns. I may choose to consult my partner, but I am quite capable on my own."

Repeat the process until you have a new message for each old message that no longer fits you. Language is extremely powerful, so pay special attention to how you phrase your new messages. Be sure to keep them in strong, positive language, using only the present tense. Even if you are not where you want to be yet, let your language reflect that future goal as if it already exists. "I am capable of planning for my financial future" is much more powerful than "I am getting better at planning for my financial future."

Keep this list of new messages handy. Post it where you see it often. Repeat your messages each time you feel yourself slipping back into your old patterns. Change will come, so stick with it!

### Eleanor's Story

Somestimes women from our workshops will let us know about the long-term effects of the work they started with us. Eleanor told us about her experience.

I had some difficulty at first with rewriting my money messages. But I kept at it, even carrying around a small notebook so I could write down things that popped into my head. I kept the two lists, confident that if I didn't immediately know how to rewrite an old belief, eventually I would.

Sure enough, that's what has happened over the past six months. It's much easier to come up with new beliefs now that I have the hang of it. My biggest stumbling block was believing that I didn't deserve to make my own decisions about money. I realized that it came from an old family message—I was living out what my mother had lived. But finding a new belief was quite a challenge. That message had impacted on my life in so many ways, giving rise to a number of other negative beliefs. I had to sort through those before I got to that fundamental message. Once I realized what was at the bottom of so many of my unhealthy beliefs, I could face it head-on and replace it with what I truly now believe—that I'm deserving and capable of making excellent decisions about money.

I can't begin to tell you how much freer I feel. My husband has been a little surprised by some of the steps I've taken, but I think he realizes he better be supportive! He knows I mean business. I never thought I could be this successful dealing with my money issues. I might have other negative messages that crop up from time to time, but I'm not going to let that bother me. I know how to deal with them.

## Redefining Your Relationship With Money

We need to redefine our relationship with money—this message, of course, runs throughout this book. Money is not the enemy, nor is it a friend. It is simply a tool. Nothing more and nothing less. As a wise woman named Debra told us, "We don't depend on money, money depends on us." In other words, each of us defines money and can experience it as a master or, as Debra suggests, as a servant.

How can we bring ourselves to the point where we are able to acknowledge that truth and act on it? Following are some steps to take in becoming more powerful when relating to money.

## Step One: Taking the Emotion Out of the Issue

One of the most difficult aspects of redefining our relationship with money is learning to take the emotion out of the issue. Notice we said it is difficult, not impossible. Not only can it be done, but it is also a change you can make that will pay huge dividends. By now you can probably list the emotions that handicap you regarding money. Fear, self-doubt, stress, worry, feelings of inadequacy, and lack of confidence may be some of the items on your personal list of negative emotions surrounding money.

Take a minute to mentally review your inventory of handicapping emotions surrounding money. List and number them here:

_____

_____

_____

Now look back over your list. For each emotion you noted, write in the following space how it keeps you from taking care of yourself financially. For example, Jodie listed fear as her major handicapping emotion. When she thought about how it kept her from taking care of herself financially, she wrote, ``When I feel the fear, I become frozen in time and space. I don't move. So I don't make any decisions about my money.'' Write here how your emotions affect you:

_____

_____

_____

Next, think of one lesson to be learned from each emotion. Again, using fear as an example, you might respond similarly to Lori: ''I am given many opportunities to learn about myself and work through my fears. Money is one of many teaching tools for me as I learn to walk through fear.'' Write your lesson(s) in the space provided:

_____

_____

_____

Completing this short exercise will raise your awareness level so that you will now find it difficult to fall back into the same old emotions without noticing them. Awareness is power. Here's how to make that power work for you:

The next time you are confronted with a money issue, pay attention to the emotions surrounding it. As you notice the old emotions, select a muscle somewhere in your body and tighten it. You may also make a tight fist if that feels more appropriate. Repeat to yourself as you squeeze that muscle, ''I am taking my emotions out of this.'' Then release the tension. Do it a second time. Tighten then release, tighten then release.

If you practice this exercise every time you are aware of emotional involvement about money, at least two things will happen. First, by acknowledging the emotion and focusing on it, you allow yourself to take control. You are less likely to feel overwhelmed and out of control. Second, you will find that the emotion becomes manageable and you can utilize your rational side. Any time you are able to reclaim your personal power, you reap the benefits of confidence and sureness.

## *Jennifer's Story*

I can tell you where I run into a bunch of emotions about money—in the grocery store. I'm much better than I was, but I used to hate buying groceries. I didn't have much money, so it was scary for me to be putting items in my cart, trying to keep a mental tally, and fearing all the time that I would get to the checkout stand and not have enough money. I can remember as a child sometimes having to take something back and put it on the shelf because we didn't have enough money to pay the total. I would be so embarrassed I just wanted to run out of the store.

But I felt like my mother needed me—my brother sure wasn't going shopping with her—so every week I went. I still try to shop every other week, so I know I don't have this licked. But as a young adult I realize that I put myself into the old familiar routine of being terrified as I pushed that cart up to the checkout. I always felt great relief when I could pay the bill.

With my last raise, it finally dawned on me that I am quite capable of supporting myself, including paying for my groceries. I know my old fears have no logical basis, yet I need to be vigilant about my feelings as I put things into my cart. Some part of me wants to get out my calculator and keep a running total. But another part wants to buy whatever I feel like buying and damn the price. I knew I reached a breakthrough last week when I put some expensive chocolates and a bag of shrimp into my cart and didn't feel queasy about it. I know myself well enough to know that I'm not going to overspend. As long as I keep reminding myself of that, I can keep away from those old fears.

## Step Two: Work to Understand Money

That which we fear becomes less fearsome when we know something about it. If we have a fear of flying on airplanes, for instance, one way to dispel that fear is to learn more about flying. Perhaps we could learn about how pilots are trained. Maybe we can read the safety records of commercial airline flights. When we do our research, we are relieved to find that, statistically, we face more danger driving a car around in most cities than we do in an airplane. This may not totally eliminate our fear, but it goes a long way toward controlling it. We are less likely to fear that which is known. Information lessens fear and brings us control.

This same principle works in dealing with our money issues. The more we know, the less mysterious the whole subject is, and the more manageable it becomes. Here are some ways you can become knowledgeable about money management and your financial life:

• *Read books.* Find books in the library or the bookstore that present a clear, straightforward approach to money management. You may wish to look for books written by women for women, but don't limit yourself. There are many good books written by men as well. Find one that works for you and presents the information you need in a way you understand. Begin to envision yourself acting on this knowledge.

• *Read magazines.* Familiarize yourself with some of the finance and money management magazines written specifically for a lay audience. There are many good ones out there. You may wish to spend an afternoon at your public library just browsing through their selection to help you find a magazine written in a style that appeals to you.

Even if you find the reading a little boring at first, stick with it—as you become more familiar with words and terms, you will find it more interesting. Again, knowledge will help your interest grow. Continue imagining yourself using this information.

• *Take advantage of freebies.* Many financial institutions give free workshops and seminars for novice investors. Attend, even if you are not ready to invest. You will increase your familiarity with financial terms and practices. Many of these seminars and workshops are given with the goal of pitching to potential investors, so be wary of signing up for anything you don't absolutely want. The idea is to take back your power regarding money. Financial institutions and brokerage houses sometimes give out free brochures and handbooks. Again, take advantage of this opportunity, at the same time being cautious about committing yourself to a commercial service that may not fit for you. You can gather much good, free information in this way. Use it to become more informed and you will develop confidence in your new knowledge.

• *Take a class.* Your local community college may have a class on personal finance, or you may find just what you need through a community-based, noncredit institution. Find a course that fits your price range. Attend all sessions of the class. Don't allow yourself to be intimidated if it appears that everyone in the class knows more than you do. In the first place, it probably isn't true. We often go into a new situation with the feeling of being the dumbest person in the whole group. Second, even if you are the least knowledgeable person there, so what? You need to start somewhere, so just hang in. It will get easier and you will catch on. Besides, a good instructor will want you to learn and will give you help and encouragement.

• *Talk to others.* Begin to discuss money issues with your friends and family. Talk about what you are learning in your classes and from your readings. Get ideas about what other people do with their investments, which bank has the best deal on a checking account, which financial planners work especially well with women. Use an informal information network to gather information to help you become more knowledgeable. As you talk about money issues, you also gain practice in breaking the taboo that says it's not ladylike to be interested in or talk about money.

• *Reclaim your power.* As women, many of us have given away our power where money is concerned. We have allowed ourselves to be less knowledgeable in this aspect of our lives than any other. We have either given responsibility over to someone else or have simply ignored the issue altogether. The time has come to reclaim your power.

Think about one thing you can do this week to better understand how money works. Complete this sentence:

This week I will increase my knowledge about money by _____
_____.

Remember, the journey of a thousand steps is taken one step at a time.

### *Carol Lynn's Story*

I never planned on being divorced and it certainly wasn't something I chose. I was angry about having to take charge of my life. Every time I had to do something that my ex-husband used to take care of, I would say a lot of unkind things about him. That didn't do me any good, so I finally started talking with my cousin. I've always admired the way she handles her life and the kinds of decisions she makes, so she seemed like a good support. She was never judgmental about what I was doing or my lack of knowledge. And she's given me some good advice.

I got the house in the divorce because I have the main care for my handicapped son. Being responsible for him also made me think I had to be very careful with my money. My cousin helped me realize I was using that as an excuse for not doing anything. Still, I remember going to see a financial planner for the first time. I was so nervous. But I found it easier than I thought it would be. She asked me all the right questions—what were my goals and needs, even how I felt about investing. She guided me into refinancing to get a lower mortgage rate.

Refinancing turned out to be another adventure. I knew nothing. But by this time, I was determined to learn. I didn't care if someone thought I was stupid, I asked every question I had. If I didn't understand the response, I asked again. I remember how excited I got when I finally understood what a point is! So now I'm enthusiastic about learning and taking charge of my life. I feel more confident than ever that I can make a financially sound life for both my son and me.

Once in a while I think about my ex-husband and I wish he were here to handle all this. Then I remember that when he was supposed to be doing all this stuff with money, he wasn't. He could dawdle more than anyone I know. The other day I was feeling kind of sorry for myself when I realized that I'm doing a much better job of this than he ever did. I don't think I'll be pitying myself any more.

## Step Three: Resolve to Take Charge of Your Money Life Now

Don't wait until the "right time" to begin redefining your relationship with money. Start now, even if it's just a small step like resolving to balance your checkbook every month so you always know what's in your account. Small steps lead to bigger ones. Waiting for the right time only leads to inaction because it gives us the perfect excuse for procrastination.

As counselors, we frequently encourage our clients to "act as if" when they are developing new behaviors—that is, we suggest they act as if the behavior they strive for is already within their grasp. Similarly, we encourage you to visualize yourself acting on information as you acquire it to make your learning more concrete. We also know that action follows thought—if you act as if, you will.

For example, you might ask yourself, "What would a person in charge of her money life do now?" Well, a person in charge of her money life would definitely know the amount in her checkbook at any given time. Thus, if we are acting as if, we want to keep our checkbook balanced. The answer gives us guidance and we can then act out this new behavior.

Acting as if we are in charge of our money lives requires us to move to a new level of competence. As thought leads to action, action then becomes habit. We don't have to wait until we are in charge of our financial life in order to act as if we are.

Begin now to act as if you are in charge of your money life. When Kay explained the act-as-if concept to a young woman in therapy, the woman first looked puzzled as she tried to place the idea in a framework that worked for her. Quickly, her face brightened with recognition as she said, "Oh! You mean fake it 'til you make it!" Act as if or fake it 'til you make it. Either way, it works.

## Emily's Story

Although my husband has always handled our money and encouraged me to take part, I used to resist. I'd find any excuse not to participate. I think I was kind of scared to get involved. But I finally realized that this wasn't very smart. I needed to know about our finances. We started by sharing the bill-paying responsibilities along with balancing the checkbook. As I got comfortable with that, I became more involved in our investments. I learned to read the annual reports and my husband explained his rationale for choosing certain stocks over others.

I read a magazine article and realized that I needed to establish credit in my own name. So I took a giant leap and got my own charge card. I trust my husband, but that doesn't mean that I'm going to continue leaving everything up to him. Now we discuss what to invest in and I can hold up my end of the conversation. I even did some research and found a better checking account—one that pays interest. We switched. I must say that I'm enjoying my new confidence about money a lot more than I ever thought I would.

## Heads Up: We See More Clearly With Our Heads Out of the Coins

Whether we bury our heads in the sand or the coins, the result is the same: We remain unable to act on our own behalf. This fearful behavior deprives us of the opportunity to look outside ourselves for resources that could enlighten and assist us. More important, we neglect to tap into our inner resources, those same strengths that have gotten us through countless other tough situations. By denying ourselves the chance to face down our fears, we remain stuck and unable to grow. What a price to pay for a false security!

A social worker describes her ideal relationship to money as "Recognizing that money is a means to an end, not the end itself." This is a worthy goal as we strive to redefine our money relationship.

We encourage you to continue to work through your own unique brand of head-in-the-coins behavior. Give yourself the opportunity to look around you, face down your money dragons, and act in a positive, healthful manner.

Ellen, a sales manager turned writer, defined financial security as "loving yourself enough and trusting yourself enough to know that you can rely on yourself and take care of yourself no matter what happens." This definition can serve as a guide as we work through our money issues. Without trust in ourselves, we find it impossible to grow, take risks, and develop more confident behaviors. We need to learn that we can indeed trust ourselves.

Like the ostrich, we have the strength, ability, and inner resources to survive and thrive without resorting to the false security of burying our heads and hiding in fear. The time has come to take our heads out of the coins, look around, and make plans to control our financial lives. We can do it.

# $\mathcal{T}$o Give It Away or Not to Give It Away

Having a clear relationship with money means accepting a new level of self-power. This is one of the underlying themes of this book. We've examined many messages that keep us from this power. We have also outlined exercises to assist you in redesigning your negative messages so you can enter into a full partnership with money. We hope you are feeling much more positive about and in control of money.

Now we want to examine two facets of how women relate to money that fall under the notion: Do I give it away or not? And if I don't give it away, how much do I charge? By "it" we mean both money and work because money is commonly generated by our labors. These questions bring up the delicate issues of examining motivations for charitable giving, taking responsibility for our money, and asking for what our work is worth in the marketplace. The dilemma about giving it away or not giving it away can trip up women in many subtle ways. By getting caught in its web, women can sabotage themselves and other women, often without realizing it. First let's look at giving it away and then explore the issue of asking for a fair price for our work.

# Giving It Away

## Charitable Giving

One of the most insidious notions keeping us in a depowered position with money is the "virtuous" idea that giving money away is better than learning how to relate to it. We've all heard the saying, "'Tis better to give than to receive." While the intention of this idea is usually one of encouraging charity, it can also imply that receiving money isn't good. Far from encouraging charity based on empowerment for all concerned, this message can be used to avoid learning about the realities about money—if we give it away, we don't have to learn what to do with it. Some women "give" money away by spending it, and others literally give it away to other people or to charities. While we don't want to discourage charitable donations, we do want to look at the motivation behind the giving, regardless of the form.

What is important in this dynamic is that the intention for the giving is clear. When we give from a place of getting rid of, we devalue ourselves and our gift. What may look like a noble act of charity has become, underneath it all, an avoidance of financial responsibility. One of the most powerful messages that feeds into this scenario is the admonishment that if we don't give, give, give, then we're selfish. And, as every woman knows, selfish is BAD. We can't be nice if we're selfish. We can't be good if we're selfish. This powerful message pervades our psyches.

Did you get the message that giving is always good and being selfish is bad? If so, what is the exact wording of it? Write it down so you are clear about it.

---

---

There are a number of negative outcomes that can result when behavior is motivated by a fear of being selfish. Codependency tops the list, followed by lack of assertiveness and indirect communication. The individual involved seldom, if ever, gets her needs met, but at the same time she tends to everyone else's needs. Thus, she lives in constant resentment. She may give to others, but she has difficulty feeling any deep joy in that giving. She is very busy taking care of every one else while she neglects her own Self. Remember the analogy in Chapter 6 of putting the oxygen mask on yourself before putting it on your children? It's a good image to keep in mind as you consider your motivations for giving.

We would like to encourage women caught in this dilemma to consider the notion of "healthy selfishness." This concept revolves around the idea that in order to be charitable with someone else, we must first be charitable with ourselves. Only by replenishing our energy will we have any to give, whether that energy comes in the form of fixing a meal, listening compassionately, or writing a check. Women often have challenges about accepting nurturing. We're more conditioned to give it than to receive it. And there's a parallel in that conditioning with how we deal with money.

One way to begin breaking out of behaviors that are rooted in a fear of being selfish is to ask, "What is the healthy thing for me to do right now?" Focusing on making choices that nourish our well-being will keep us clearer about our behaviors. It will guide us away from fear-based behaviors and toward choices that are derived from our strengths.

For example, suppose you've had an exhausting day and you just want to take some time for yourself. Then your partner asks you for a back massage. If the "fear of being seen as selfish" tape starts running in your head, you will put aside your needs and give your partner that back massage. Exhausted and in need of rest and rejuvenation, you put out even more energy, making yourself even more exhausted. But if you take a moment to ask yourself, "What is healthy for me to do right now?" you will likely answer that you need first to recharge your own batteries before giving to someone else. Taking care of ourselves means we have more to share with others, not less. The same holds true for our relationship with money: Giving it away in order to avoid a positive relationship with it is not healthy. And it's a sure-fire way to deplete our financial resources.

Taking our power back in dealing with issues about giving our money away means we have examined our motivations and are clear with the negative messages we may have acquired. Our charitable giving empowers the receiver and gives us a deep sense of satisfaction. We are embracing our money power, not avoiding it. Take a look at what you wrote down as your message that giving is always good and being selfish is bad. Now create a positive message for yourself that embraces healthy selfishness and your money power. Write it here:

_____

_____

_____

_____

_____

## Joycelyn's Story

In the midst of a workshop, Joycelyn had an uncomfortable realization. She explained:

> I've always been the one in the office who put together the birthday celebrations and the going-away parties. Anytime a coworker thinks we should have a gathering, I'm always the one who is asked to be in charge. And I enjoy that. I mean, I think it's important for us to have these little get-togethers. I do everything—set the theme, buy the refreshments and the gift, and make sure everyone has a good time.

What I just realized, though, is that I think I've been letting myself be used. I try to collect the money to pay for all this before the event, but there are always some people who don't have the money when I ask for it. It's usually the same people. So a lot of the time, I'm short and I have to put more of my own money in. I don't want to seem cheap, so I've never said anything. I figure those people who didn't pay know they didn't, so they should just give me the money. I've never felt comfortable asking them a second time. I mean, I don't want people to think I'm a nag.

But I just realized that I've been letting my coworkers use me. And it's my fault. I thought I was being a good person, but now I see that my "charity" has really been misplaced. Plus, I've allowed others to avoid their responsibility because I've let them off the hook. Next time there's a birthday in the office, someone else can organize it!

## Unconditional Giving

Another concept that is important in dealing with the giving-it-away dilemma is that of unconditional giving. Too often we learn just the opposite—that giving has strings attached. This belief works both ways. If we give conditionally, then we are expecting something in return and we may or may not be disappointed. Conversely, if we are on the receiving end, we may assume that something is expected of us. Then we feel obligated to give back. Either way, the giving and the receiving are muddied by conditions and expectations. Regardless of where we may find ourselves, whether giving with strings or receiving with strings, neither feels good.

On the other hand, unconditional giving means that the gift is given freely, with no expectation of receiving anything in return. Anything, that is, except the positive feelings we have when we give from clear intention. When we give from this kind of motivation, the receiver is free to respond however she chooses. She knows, consciously or subconsciously, that there are no conditions attached to the gift. Therefore, she is free to do with the gift what she wants. And she is not restricted by any sense of obligation to the giver. So we need to look at whether or not we are giving unconditionally.

## Leah's Story

I learned my lesson about conditional giving after I got divorced. My ex-husband never gave me a gift unless it was my birthday or Christmas. He just wasn't into giving me flowers or a card for no particular reason. When he traveled on business, I never got anything. After our divorce, I began dating someone who was just the opposite. At first it was great. I'd get flowers delivered at work. He would show up for a date with a present for me. Some of these were rather expensive pieces of jewelry. I was so flattered.

But as time went on, I began to realize that there was an undercurrent of expectation. I couldn't put my finger on it at first, but I was feeling more and more uncomfortable. I came to realize that the gifts were a substitute for emotion. He had great expectations about what I was supposed to give emotionally but didn't seem to feel the need to give to me at a feeling level. Finally, I asked him to stop giving me so many presents. He seemed offended at first and continued trying to give me things. When I told him I didn't want his things but that I wanted his love, he split.

So he taught me a lot about conditional giving. Now when I give someone something, I am very clear within myself that I don't expect anything in return. And I get very uncomfortable if someone says, in response to a favor I've done, "I owe you one." I'm quick to tell them they don't owe me anything. And I really believe that.

# Not Giving It Away

## Honoring What We Have to Give

In examining our motivations behind a tendency to give it away, yet another issue can be operating. Every time we expect women to work for less than the going market rate, we devalue their work. This is true whether we are hiring someone for a full-time position or for a temporary, contracted position, or asking someone to give a talk. Most businesswomen have been approached by women's groups that expect them to virtually give away their services. We're being disloyal to "the cause" or nonsupportive of women's groups if we fail to lower our fees or to do something "pro bono." Have you had this happen to you?

Every time a woman is asked to give away her services under these conditions, she is being told that her work isn't valued or that if she expects her work to have the same value as a man's, she's being selfish. If a woman doesn't comply with these demands, she may be ostracized and rebuked for not supporting women's causes. Yet, paradoxically, those same women are not supporting *her!* And the woman being put upon to make this choice becomes party to the devaluing of her work when she agrees, *knowing in her gut that she ought to be paid in full.* But she doesn't want to be accused of not supporting women's issues; she doesn't want to be seen as selfish. So she makes her decision based on these fears, giving up a part of herself in a situation that dismisses and devalues her and her work. We have encountered this kind of discrimination at both the local and national levels. Why women do this to each other is a puzzle.

Bear in mind that we're not talking about those times when

women give freely of their time and talent—a recent poll by the National Foundation for Women Business Owners found that 78 percent of women business owners spend some time volunteering, compared to 48 percent of all adults.[1] What we are focusing on here is the diminishing of women's work by other women who *expect* to be the beneficiary of that work without paying a fair market price. And we want to look at the motivations of women who work for less than the going market rate. When this is done from a clear relationship with money, then the outcome will be healthy for everyone. But if women decide to work for less from a place of low self-esteem or of not knowing how to ask for what their work is worth, then the outcome will likely be less than positive.

Decisions made for unhealthy reasons serve no one. The giver feels put upon, perhaps even resentful. She may be upset with herself for once again allowing herself to be taken advantage of. She may discover, too late, that her giving had conditions attached. The receiver knows at a deep level what has happened—in devaluing one woman's work, all women's work has been diminished, including her own.

We can honor women's work when, with clear motivations, we ask them to share their talents. Conversely, when we give freely of our skills and talents, we can experience joy in sharing and giving. We honor ourselves and other women's work with this attitude.

## Edith's Story

When we talk about honoring what we have to give, we know we are approaching a delicate subject. One workshop participant in particular became very upset with our ideas. Edith is a local radio personality with a weekly talk show devoted to women's issues. She had told everyone at the outset that she didn't have any money issues, that she was taking the workshop as research for her show. We were somewhat surprised to see her because she had contacted us ahead of time requesting that she be allowed to attend for free. We weren't totally certain that she accepted our explanation about valuing women's work when we said no to her request.

Edith flatly stated that she could not afford to have her show if she had to pay women to be on. She couldn't, she insisted, even pay for long distance phone calls when she interviewed someone from out of town. That woman was getting valuable publicity, Edith explained, so she should be willing to pay the charges. As she continued, we observed the other participants becoming increasingly uneasy. Finally, one of them spoke up.

"It seems to me that you're just using these women. Sure, they may get some publicity, but what makes you think they're any better off than you are? You're getting advertising revenues, aren't you? I don't think you would be doing that show for nothing. Besides, every time you insist that you can't afford something, you put yourself in a vulnerable position."

Another woman added, "You make yourself a victim of your own unwillingness to take charge of your money issues when you continue to undervalue other women's work. Don't you understand that until you value their work, you won't value your own?"

As the rest of the women nodded their agreement, we sat quietly while Edith took in what the others were saying to her. Finally her defenses seemed to crack as she said, "I never saw it that way. I guess I have some thinking to do."

## How Much Do I Charge?

So once we've decided not to give it away, how do we know how much to charge? If we lock into the belief that receiving money is not good, we can dodge the issue of asking for what our work is worth in the marketplace.

While we discussed this issue earlier (Chapter 3), we revisit it here from a different perspective. A consultant made the importance of resolving this issue clear when she told us, "We don't get paid what we ask for, we get paid what we think we're worth."

Women often have difficulty putting a price tag on our work; we have seldom been taught how to do this. We often have difficulty asking for a raise or charging an appropriate amount of money for our work. We believe that the quality of our work should be apparent to the boss, so we shouldn't have to assert ourselves in this regard. Or we're sure that somehow the marketplace will simply know the value of our work and will pay accordingly.

Furthermore, since women are giving away their work below the market value, they expect other women to do the same. In business dealings, they may even expect men to charge higher prices than women and are shocked when some women don't live up (or down) to this expectation. The result is the dismissal of women's work by society, by other women, and by ourselves, accompanied by lost income. Being confused about asking for what our work is worth has many ramifications.

Diane had an incident happen to her a number of years ago that brought this point home, although it took her a while to understand what had happened. She was just starting out in her consulting business and had agreed to do a workshop at the local community college. The person who hired her was a friend. Diane agreed to a reduced fee because the work was for a nonprofit institution. A few weeks after the first presentation, her friend asked her to do a second one but offered her less than half the previous reimbursement. Diane explained that she had already reduced her fee and could not work for less. Her friend became irritated and told her that several other women had agreed to present for the much lower fee. She implied that because they were willing to work for such a low rate, Diane ought to as well. This incident not only ended Diane's work for that friend, it ended the friendship as well. In reflecting on this later, Diane wondered if this woman would have expected a man to work for the $10 being offered. Probably not.

Consider how you feel about asking for what you are worth. How do you feel about negotiating for a certain salary? How did you respond to this statement on the questionnaire? It brought out a wide range of responses during our research for the book. And many of those statements were loaded with emotion. One woman spoke for many when she questioned, "Who sets the standard of what I am worth? Who makes the decision as to how much my education, life experiences, intuition, inner strength, and the ability to make great banana bread is worth?"

Too often, we become caught in society's message that the amount of money we earn defines our worth as individuals. So when we are asked how much our work is worth, we may feel as if we're saying how much value we personally have. This is a totally incorrect understanding of money. Remember: Money is simply a means of exchange. We engage in work and we accept money in return for that work. The amount of money may reflect our abilities, accomplishments, recognized expertise, or the ease with which we can be replaced. But it *never* reflects our worth as individuals. We honor the challenge many women experience in accepting this belief. As a business owner told us, "I know intellectually that my worth is not related to money but psychologically my worth is linked to my ability to produce income."

As we have already noted, the phrase "asking for what you're worth" stirs a range of responses from women. And age does not seem to be a factor. Women in their sixties and in their twenties have told us similar things. A woman in her mid-twenties said, "This would be a problem for me. I tend to not be assertive in this area." A middle-aged woman voiced her opinion about the source of the difficulty: "Women are taught to settle for less than men." A successful saleswoman flatly stated that she can't ask for what she's worth. She admitted, "I feel worthless too often." Cynthia, a college instructor, said, "I'm not sure what I'm worth."

These comments speak to the need to clearly rid ourselves of the idea that the amount of money we earn indicates our self-worth. If we didn't hear this message in our family, we certainly have been bombarded with it in society. It's very difficult to keep this idea from impacting on our self-esteem. An art instructor wrote that asking for what she is worth is very hard for her. She said, "It has felt like I am a minority person not listened to in the white male-dominated outer world." A college student noted, "I am constantly questioning my worth."

Then there are the homemakers who don't collect *any* salary. Barbara, describing herself as a homemaker, vision keeper, and sometimes mystic, expressed the frustration many women seem to have on this subject: "I feel that right now I am engaged in one of the most important jobs on the planet at this time—that is my spiritual work—that is raising whole healthy female children not numbed by the culture. If I were paid what I'm worth I would be making as much as Michael Jordan, but I'm not. It is such an obscene game. When I think of it I have a lot of anger and powerless feeling toward a society as screwed up as ours."

At the heart of this issue is something women often find difficult—separating who we are from what we do. For example, when women create, during part of the process we are often totally identified with the thing being created.[2] The creator and created are one. This close attachment can make putting a price tag on our work feel as if we are labeling our own worth. Fortunately, our creative process also gives us the opportunity to separate from what we are creating. Gaining emotional distance from our work at the appropriate time is a healthy and necessary part of making that work marketable.

We often have heard women talk about being unable to release their hold on some creative work in order to put it out to the public; they believe they couldn't handle the criticism. In this feeling state, they probably shouldn't make it public—they are still too attached. And they certainly shouldn't put a price tag on it. Yet when we allow the creative process to run its full course, a time will come when the creator detaches from the work. We often experience this state as boredom. Sound familiar? At this point, we usually become interested in doing something new. Now the time is right for taking the work public. Now we can attach the price tag.

We can facilitate moving toward this place of detachment by sharing our projects with supportive people when our instincts tell us that the time is right. Sometimes we need to ask the other person not to respond. We've all had the experience of sharing a new idea with someone, only to have that person respond negatively. This usually kills the idea. Our creations need to be nurtured and brought out into the open at the right time.

Carefully select the individual with whom you will share and check with your inner instincts, your "gut reaction," about the timing. Once you have taken this step, you will know if you are ready to make the creation more generally known. This might be presenting an idea to your boss, sending a manuscript to a publisher, giving a workshop, or asking for a raise. The point is, once we have separated emotionally from our creation, putting a price on it is much easier. We are less apt to confuse pricing the creation with pricing ourselves.

Another factor that makes it challenging to determine our work's worth is that women tend to define themselves in many roles and capacities, yet few of them have to do with money. So when we are asked to put a tangible value on our work, we struggle. We don't want to buy into the societal belief that how much we earn is a statement of our individual worth. At the same time, however, when we fail to appropriately value our work, we underprice ourselves in the marketplace and put ourselves at risk of losing financially as well as emotionally. When we don't have a clear idea of our market worth, we can give our work away in a dismissive and depowering way. This behavior serves no one. So being clear about the monetary value of our work and about what we are willing to accept in exchange for that work is important to our overall health—financial and emotional.

## Sorting Out the Dilemma

Again, we respect this struggle about the issues involved in giving it away or not giving it away. It's an important one for women. The challenge is threefold:

- Charging what our work is worth
- Paying other women what their work is worth in the marketplace
- Staying free of the notion that money defines our worthiness as an individual

The last notion is extremely important, especially for women like Barbara who chose to remain in the home, not earning money in the outside world.

Society gives us many messages that make tackling this challenge difficult. Women's work, regardless of the particular field, has been undervalued and underappreciated. At the same time, society tells us that our worth is determined by how much money we make. The media, especially advertising, is loaded with subtle and overt messages equating money with worth. Women have also been encouraged to volunteer, an activity that can bring mixed messages about contributing to the improvement of society and about work not having a monetary value in the marketplace. Compounding these factors is the reality that, as a group, women's time in the workforce has been relatively short. So we are still learning to value our own work as well as each other's.

We often have heard from women entrepreneurs about their struggle in resolving the dilemma of charging what they're worth. Usually these women describe a lot of discomfort at first, but they are motivated by the need to generate money to support themselves and their children. One woman said she practiced stating her desired salary out loud to herself in front of a mirror. This practice helped build her courage as well as her belief in the monetary value of her work. We encourage you to try doing this the next time you ask for a raise or negotiate a salary. It's a powerful technique. Joyce, a consultant, summed up her progression in resolving this issue when she said, "It was harder to ask for $500 a day than it is to ask for $4,000 per day."

We want to be clear that we are talking about women determining a fair exchange of money for their work. We are not including many other important factors such as satisfaction, fulfillment, or a sense of contributing something worthwhile or beautiful. Those qualities cannot—and in most cases should not—have a price tag because the intrinsic value is too subjective to quantify. Yet we want to acknowledge these aspects of work. Certainly they are important. While some people do work just for the money, most people do not. At the same time, the current reality of our society is that individuals need money to survive. And our workplace is structured such that the people in it are expected to have a clear idea of the monetary worth of their work.

Once we can reconcile to this reality, we can determine a fair rate of exchange for our work and proceed accordingly. Certainly we've all known people who have decided that they are worth $80,000 per year. Yet the reality of the workplace is that their work, given the type of work, education, and years of experience, can reasonably be exchanged for $25,000 per year. An extreme overestimate of the value of one's work may indicate some issues related to low self-esteem. Or it may simply be lack of information. What do other people in a similar situation earn?

When someone experiences a wide gulf between what she believes her work to be worth and what the market will pay, she needs to reconcile this difference somehow. If she doesn't, she will become increasingly frustrated with her work and angry with herself. If there are self-esteem issues involved, counseling may be in order. Other factors may be influencing her as well. She may simply need to gain a more widespread professional reputation, making herself more visible in the marketplace, to earn a higher fee. That may take some time and it may mean charging lower fees at the start. Or the physical location may be playing into the market price. Someone who has performed a certain kind of work in one city may find, on relocating, that her work is paid at a lower rate in her new home. So somehow the individual must reconcile this circumstance.

We often hear people talk about being "owned" by the company they work for. This unfortunate perspective feeds a feeling of being depowered and victimized. In fact, the employees have agreed to *rent* themselves to the company for a certain number of hours a day and an agreed upon number of days per year. In exchange, the company gives the employees money and, possibly, other benefits. Seeing this arrangement as a rental agreement gives the power back to the individual, freeing her to view money as an exchange for services. Her work is rented, not owned.

Reminding herself that income does not equal personal worth is much easier with this perspective. A focus on intrinsic elements also helps. A movement therapist told us, "In 85 percent of the situations, I ask for what I'm worth. If I agree on less I see a benefit other than money that makes up the difference."

Finally, in acknowledging that asking for what you're worth is important, a psychotherapist wrote, "There have been times when I have measured my professional self-esteem by my fees and yearly income—I'm glad to have grown up."

Staying clear with yourself about your motivations for charitable giving, about pricing your work, and honoring other women's work will move you toward a more positive relationship with money. Every step you have taken toward this way of relating to money also moves you closer to redefining what money means to you.

# Part Four
## Redesigning Your Relationship With Money

## Chapter Ten

# ℳoving in a New Direction

Now that you have worked to rid yourself of old, unhealthy money messages, wiping the slate clean, you are ready to move into a redesigned relationship with money. In these next chapters, we introduce you to new concepts regarding money that can keep you in a positive relationship with it. This chapter is designed to help you resolve issues you may have that are tied to fear and power. In Chapter 11, we examine the role your Inner Self plays in maintaining your new belief system and encourage you to clean up any remaining negative messages. Then we explore the concept of money as energy in Chapter 12, a notion that literally blows away all previous ideas about what money is and isn't, and in Chapter 13 we ask you to consider money in its spiritual aspect, a concept that many people find challenging to accept. We look at money messages in the workplace in Chapter 14, and, in Chapter 15, discuss how to reconcile your new relationship with money with the money value system at work. Finally, in Chapters 16 and 17, we explore exactly how your life might look as you act in accordance with your new beliefs, make some suggestions about how to assist our daughters in developing a healthy relationship with money, and examine some possible next steps.

## Time to Review

Now would be a good time to review what you've done up to this point and reflect on all that you have accomplished. We want to make sure all negative messages have been cleared out before we begin writing and adopting new money beliefs. Take a look at your genogram. Read over the family messages you uncovered in doing that work. Do any of those messages still hook you in, or can you read them over and feel nothing pulling at your gut? If you feel at ease, you know you are rid of them. If twinges remain, review some of the suggested exercises and select the one(s) that would help you to neutralize the message. Try saying the messages out loud for an added dimension. Do the same with the societal messages—review them for any remaining pull and get rid of those that still influence you.

We realize this journey has held its challenges. We know of several women who specifically asked us for questionnaires and then did not fill them out. One woman even asked for a second one only to admit that she could not bring herself to face her issues on paper. When we suggested that she might like to simply answer the questions for herself, thinking that perhaps she was reluctant to share her money messages with us, she shook her head in the negative. "I just can't face it," she said. There's a heroic aspect to being willing to confront the uncomfortable messages residing within yourself and then clearing them out. Clearing out your money messages takes some effort; reconceptualizing and redefining money takes an open mind.

## Money and Personal Transformation

One aspect of this experience that is probably very clear to you at this point is that money can be a vehicle for personal transformation. As you have eliminated old messages, you have also gotten rid of behaviors that no longer serve you regarding money. You may have made shifts in your personal relationships, moving away from people who still carry unhealthy messages about money or who relate to it in negative ways. Family relationships may have changed as you divest yourself of long-held familial messages and replaced them with your chosen beliefs. You may have experienced some unsettling situations at work as you realize how much you have changed while your organization's value system has not. (More on this situation in Chapter 14.) When financial events don't progress as we would like them to, we can abandon our new beliefs, resorting to blaming or other negative behaviors. Or we can see the situation as an indicator that we still have some unresolved issues about money. Our experience is all in our perspective. And we control our experience by controlling our perspective. We must believe we are capable of establishing a new relationship with money before we can actually accomplish it.

Remember that what happens to us financially supports our beliefs about money. Events let us know about any areas we have yet to clear out and resolve. So when an unexpected situation happens concerning money, ask yourself, "How is this event supporting my beliefs about money?" The answer to this question will provide you with information you need to clear out any residual ideas you have about money that you no longer want. This question is especially important to ask when another individual seems to be central to the financial event.

For example, we have observed that child support payments are often used to control. Diane once had a client who normally dealt with the world from a positive place of being empowered. But once a month, she would arrive for her appointment very depowered. Her encounters with her ex-husband over the monthly support payments were hard for her to recover from. In every one of those interactions, the client was giving her power over to him almost at the outset. They had a long-established pattern of this kind of interaction. Her unconscious belief was that he should hold the power with regard to money. The ex-husband would always wait until the last minute, then insist on bringing the check in person. This contact helped perpetuate their unhealthy cycle of her giving up her power to him. An argument would always ensue about the lateness of the check or the well-being of the children or her inability to manage money. All of these issues resulted in her giving up her power and admitting, one way or the other, that he still ruled in the realm of money.

Our self-power is centered on the connection between our heart and our power center located at the solar plexus. Every time the client's ex-husband would appear with the check, she would instinctively react by breaking that energy link. So Diane taught her to maintain that connection by visualizing a white-light bond between those two points. When she did this, she no longer became caught up in his manipulations. She stayed focused on her sense of self-power and became immune to his toxic behaviors. She could simply stop responding to his tirades and accusations. After a few encounters where the client stayed calm and essentially uninvolved in his efforts to pull her off center, he stopped coming to her home and began mailing the checks on time!

In experiencing the personal transformations that happen when we deal with our money messages, power is a recurring theme, as we discuss in Chapter 4. Old money messages generally depower women, encouraging them to give their power to men or to money itself! Critical to reconceptualizing and redefining money is reclaiming our power, so we want to revisit this issue one more time. The very act of saying, "I choose to define money on my terms so that it suits my needs," reclaims our power. Once women have made this change, a major economic shift is in order.

Try the following exercise to help you gain an awareness of how to maintain your sense of self-power:

Sit upright with your feet flat on the floor. Focus your attention on your heart and your solar plexus, the area just below the sternum. If you are a color person, the energy of the solar plexus is yellow and the heart energy is green. Now imagine a shaft of white light or clear water connecting those two points. Keep your focus on this connection, sensing and feeling it as strongly as you can. Breathe easily as you experience this. Give yourself five to ten minutes to experience this connection.

To reinforce your sense of self-power, repeat some of your new money messages while focusing on connecting these two points. Stay with the exercise until you feel strong and centered throughout your entire body.

Practice this exercise often so that when you need to keep your attention on your sense of self-power, you can do so easily. If you feel yourself getting pulled away from your new relationship with money and back to the old, focus your attention on your heart and your solar plexus. Maintain your attention on that connection when you have to go through a demanding encounter with another person where money is the focus or even while paying your own bills. You may find yourself less likely to become hooked into reacting in unhealthy ways. And you may even surprise yourself with what you do and say that will keep you on your path to a healthy relationship with money.

## A New Perspective on Fear

Taking our power back regarding any issue can be challenging for anyone. A common reaction to this change is fear. While we might think that people would gladly embrace their power, doing so does mean a new relationship with new behaviors, different decisions that impact beyond the individual, and a value system often at variance with the status quo. In other words, by clearing out unwanted money messages and redefining money on our terms, we become different. While we are encouraging you to make this difference healthy, it isn't always comfortable at first. So staying on track can be challenging. At this point, revisit the fears you identified in Chapter 5. We explore them in more depth here to be certain they are cleared out of your belief system.

When the subject of fear arises, we are reminded of the story from the Northwest Native population so beautifully described by Anne Cameron in *Daughters of Copper Woman*. Sisiutl is a water-born, hideous monster with heads at both ends of his body. He preys on people who cannot control their fears, feeding off the fear they generate when they see him. He seeks out people who do not know their Truth. Sisiutl is so horrifying that being afraid when he pops up is a natural response. But anyone who runs in fear will be forever trapped by that fear. The only way to escape fear's bondage is to look directly at Sisiutl—to face fear itself. The story tells us that when you face this monster, he will try to devour your face with both mouths. So each head must turn toward you. When this happens, Sisiutl sees his own face, his own Truth. Sisiutl spends his life in search of Truth. Since you have shown him his Truth, he will go, blessing you with magic. Having faced fear itself, your Truth will always be with you.

Knowing our fears can help tremendously in our search for personal transformation, in our endeavors to be free of negative beliefs that hold us back. The antidote for fear is Truth. As you confront your fears, remember this: We are born with only two fears—the fear of falling and the fear of loud noises. All other fears are learned. Somebody told you to be afraid, so you are. Let's examine some of your fears about money and changing your beliefs about money. Which ones spring to mind first? Common fears include the following: If I change, no one will like me. If I change my beliefs around money, I will have to take more risks and risks scare me. I'm afraid to go against the status quo. Do any of these sound familiar?

Write out several of your fears about changing your money beliefs:

_____

_____

_____

_____

Now think about each one of these fears. Where did you first hear it? Who gave you this fear? You probably picked it up from a family member. Perhaps you have already identified it on your genogram as part of your family money messages. Beside each message, write down the name of the person who gave you this fear. We're not trying to assign blame here or stir up unnecessary anger toward an individual. This is a kind of archeological expedition in which we want to simply identify who laid which stones in your belief system. That way, you can return the beliefs that no longer serve you. Once you have figured our where the fear came from, send it back, using some of the suggestions in Chapter 5. Mentally send the fear flying through the air, returning to its source. Or write out the fear in a letter, describing what it has done for you in your life—there may be both positives and negatives here. Then burn the letter. Or rip it up and flush it down the toilet or add it to your compost pile. You don't have to actually tell the person who gave you the fear that you are returning it. There's no need to be angry about having picked up someone else's fear. We believe that it is unlikely that anyone has intentionally instilled fears in you regarding money. Usually these messages are delivered with the belief that they will keep you safe or protected. Many people suffered financial hardship during the Great Depression. And many families are still living with the fears that experience inspired. Identifying the source of our fears is the first step in getting rid of them, in realizing they are not true for us unless we make them true.

Having given back the fear, now ask yourself, "What is my Truth?" A good look at your personal history will help you here. Perhaps your Truth is that while you get to a financial edge, you never fall off. Your Truth may be that every time you have made strides in your personal growth, you've liked yourself better. Or your Truth may be that when you challenge the status quo, you become much more creative and life gets interesting. Perhaps your Truth is that your beliefs have been adopted from others in your life and you don't yet have a clear picture of what your Truth is. If this is the case, the next several chapters will help tremendously.

Look again at each of the fears you have just listed. In each case, ask yourself what your Truth is. Write these statements here:

_____

_____

_____

_____

While fear can be crippling in the process of personal transformation, it can also be an indicator that you are on the right path. When fears crop up during your journey to redefining money, ask yourself what your Truth is. Knowing your Truth will help ease your way toward a healthy relationship with money.

This knowledge will help you avoid common traps in the transformation process. As people understand more about how their belief system came into being, they are often tempted to blame others for their negative beliefs and for events that have happened because of those unhealthy beliefs. This is the trap of living in the past. We are encouraging you to reconceptualize and redefine money so that your present and future can be the way you want it. Forgive the past, including the people who may have given you their fears as well as yourself for actions taken that you would no longer choose. Truth helps you forgive. Avoiding blame and accepting responsibility are critical in redefining money and assuming a power role in relating to money.

In this process, tune up your awareness of what you say about money and your relationship to it. One of our favorite phrases is: What you can conceive and believe, you will achieve. Your words have power. They define and describe your belief system. Listen for what you are saying about your money beliefs. What you believe is what you will achieve. For example, we encourage people to drop the phrase, "I can't afford. . . ." These frequently spoken words are loaded with the potential for blaming someone or some set of circumstances for our own perceived lack. They are depowering. Think of how often you have used these words and have heard others use them. We suggest a new phrase, one that keeps your power intact while describing your situation. "I don't want to spend my money on . . . right now." Or, "I choose not to spend my money on . . . right now."

How often have you heard the following phrases spoken by management in your workplace? "We can't afford new computers." "We can't afford to send you to that conference." "We can't afford to give you a raise." Changing the company language gives an interesting and perhaps more truthful perspective on workplace thinking. "We don't want to spend money on new computers." "We don't want to spend money on sending you to that conference." "We don't want to spend money on giving you a raise."

In our efforts to redefine money, we want our focus to be threefold:

- Developing a healthy relationship with money
- Accepting our power and eliminating fears about money
- Looking at untoward events as holding valuable information to help us clear out any residual money messages that no longer serve us

Having done your work in clearing out old messages, you are truly ready to start from scratch in developing a healthy relationship with money.

## Janis's Story

When Janis came to her first money workshop, she was reluctant to fully participate in the discussions and exercises. We remembered her as being especially argumentative when we talked about the concept of making choices as opposed to falling back on "I can't afford. . . ." To our surprise, she joined us for a second workshop about two years later. She readily told the group about her experience.

When I first came to this workshop, I fought tooth and nail to keep my old beliefs about money. I didn't realize that was what I was doing—I just thought you two were wrong and I was right. But something got through to me because the evening of that workshop, I asked my husband to take me out to eat at my favorite restaurant. You know what he said? "We can't afford it." I automatically started to agree with him, but I suddenly heard our discussion in the workshop about making choices instead of excuses. And I realized that I was mad about his response. So I told him he was just choosing not to take me out. He didn't get it, but I did.

Ever since, I've been keeping track of my money messages, especially the things I say without thinking and the things other people say that I quickly agree with. Now when I hear some negative message, I write it down and I ask myself what my Truth is. As soon as I know the answer, I write it down opposite the first message. Any time I'm tempted to fall back on some negative belief, whether it's my own or someone else's, I remind myself of what my Truth is. I feel so much freer now around money. And I also feel ready to get rid of any other negative messages I might be carrying around. I've noticed that while this was a difficult process at first, it has definitely gotten easier. I've been educating my husband, too. I don't let him get away with making negative statements about money anymore. We still don't have the money to spend on everything we think we want to do, but we have a clearer sense of where we are going with the money we do have.

## *Chapter Eleven*

# *U*nderstanding Your Inner Self

Throughout this book we've talked about your money messages. By now you probably have a very clear idea about what those messages are and where they came from in your life. We've also been guiding you toward redesigning your negative messages so you can have a more positive relationship with money. What we have been focusing on is the Inner Self, that part of the psyche that holds all of our thoughts and feelings about ourselves—who we are and what we believe.

The Inner Self begins to form the moment we start hearing about ourselves and observing how our world operates. For this reason, beliefs held in our Inner Self are both obvious and subtle. They have developed from words, actions, and feelings, from what we hear and what we see. Much of what resides in the Inner Self developed before we had the awareness to reject a belief that came from outside ourselves. So we have both positives and negatives residing within us.

If we were told something by an authority figure often enough, we eventually believed it—and that belief became embedded in our Inner Self. For example, if we were frequently told we were smart, then being intelligent became part of how we see ourselves. Conversely, if we were told we were stupid, then that message became part of our self-image, regardless of our innate intelligence.

In addition to acquired beliefs, the Inner Self also holds the

Core Self, the person we truly are, devoid of outside messages. The whole process we call personal growth is really a journey into the Inner Self for the purpose of getting rid of those beliefs that don't belong to us—the ones that fail to serve us in a positive way—and replacing them with messages that will further our health and well-being. Engaging in this journey challenges us to listen closely to the voice arising from our Core Self and to redesign our belief system in support of who we truly are as unique individuals. This ongoing process often challenges us creatively, emotionally, intellectually, and spiritually. Sound familiar?

## Discovering Your Inner Self

Exploring the Inner Self can be accomplished in many ways. We want to keep this process simple yet offer you several exercises so you can choose what works best for you. First, we suggest trying a sentence completion exercise. As we've said before, your best companion on this journey is your curiosity.

To get a sense of what's in your Inner Self, complete the following sentence as many times as you can:

I am _____.

For example, Diane might write: I am a cat lover; I am a hiker; I am a writer; I am a scuba diver; I am a speaker. Kay might write: I am a therapist; I am a book lover; I am a sister. We could go on and on, describing ourselves in relationship to others, to our work, to our passions, our fears, our accomplishments.

We encourage you to explore this exercise fully, to write down as many ``I am . . .'' statements as you can. Sometimes varying the wording can direct your awareness to different aspects of yourself. For instance, you might try completing these sentences as many times as you can:

I enjoy _____.

I believe _____

I am afraid of _____.

Be aware that the Inner Self contains both positive and negative messages. When you discover a negative message, writing it down is important. This activity helps you to acknowledge and evaluate the message—a necessary step in changing beliefs. If you try to ignore it, pushing it away mentally, it will come back, nagging at you until you recognize it.

Also, it's important as you explore your Inner Self to be supportive of yourself. That means avoiding any put-downs or criticisms you may be tempted to heap upon yourself as you discover some negative beliefs. You may find you have characteristic, habitual put-down statements like, "I'm so foolish" or "I always do. . . ." Write these down—they are part of the Inner Self, too.

You could probably write for several hours and still not be finished. We suggest that you write as much as comes to mind right now. Additional thoughts will probably arise for you during the next several days. Simply write them down so that you gain an ever increasing picture of your Inner Self.

Another approach to try in understanding your Inner Self is drawing it. Drawing can give you a new dimension in understanding yourself. You're putting your words into pictures, into symbols. You can be as representational about this drawing as you want. For example, when we do this exercise in workshops and Diane draws her Inner Self on a white board, not all participants recognize that one image she has drawn is a cat. No matter. Diane knows it's a cat. What's important about your picture of your Inner Self is that you understand what the picture means.

We recognize that many people have some negative messages about their artistic talents. But there are ways around these messages. If you get stalled by messages about your ability to draw, use your nondominant hand. We simply don't have the expectations of quality from that hand. So using it can be freeing.

We encourage you to use a large piece of paper for this exercise and have crayons or colored pencils or other drawing materials that will allow you a wide choice of colors. Take some time now to draw your Inner Self. Here's a sample of Diane's Inner Self that is meant as encouragement to you.

All of us have a hodge-podge of messages in the Inner Self, some of which are in conflict with others. It's the total picture we're striving for here. Only when we accept who we are can we move forward in our efforts to construct a more positive Inner Self.

If drawing doesn't appeal to you, make a collage of your Inner Self instead. Get a good-sized piece of poster board, one that will accept having things glued to it. Then gather together lots of old magazines, scissors, and glue. Allow yourself to use both pictures and words. Work rapidly, cutting items as they appeal to you. Try to avoid being too rational about your selections. Now arrange and paste them on your poster board in whatever way appeals to you. You may be surprised when you see what you chose to include. Have fun with this exercise!

At this point, pause to reflect on what you have learned about your Inner Self. Take a few minutes to complete the following sentence:

When I consider my Inner Self, I now know that I _____

_____.

## Money Messages and Your Inner Self

Now that you have begun to develop a clearer image of your Inner Self, you can focus on money messages residing within you. Look at your drawing or collage. Did you include any images to depict your beliefs about money? If not, add them now. Remember, these messages can be contradictory, so if you find this is the case, know that you are just being human! Using the exercises you have completed previously in this book as a guide, add your money messages to your Inner Self picture. For example, based on how you've constructed your genogram, what messages are part of your Inner Self? On the questionnaire, how did you respond to the sentence completions and to other money messages you carry with you? Consider these questions as you continue working on your picture of your Inner Self.

## Redesigning Your Inner Self

We have observed over the years that humans love to be right! Even if it makes us miserable, we insist on being right. In other words, we all behave according to what we believe to be true about ourselves.

So if we are to interact differently with money, we have to first know what our money messages are. By understanding that they are a part of our Inner Self, we can next move to redesign those messages.

The Inner Self is a very powerful force. Many studies show us that if an individual is told certain things about herself and she accepts those ideas, she will act in alignment with them. For example, if a child is told every time she trips or bumps into something that she is clumsy, her movements will become more uncoordinated. She accepts what she is told—being clumsy has become part of her Inner Self—and she then behaves according to her belief. Never mind that she was simply tripping or bumping into things in the normal course of being human. Once she accepts the "clumsy" label, she will behave as if it were true. And each time she stumbles, she will probably reinforce her conviction by saying to herself, "I sure am clumsy." Further, she will be flooded with feelings associated with being clumsy.

You may have noticed as you were going through the exercises designed to help you know your Inner Self that feelings often arise in connection with beliefs. Can you identify the feelings associated with the images you have drawn in your picture or pasted in your collage? Are they familiar? When do you usually experience them? Sometimes we are aware of the feeling without knowing what the words are that express the thought. To grasp the influence the Inner Self has on us, we need to understand that our self-concept is constructed with both a thinking and a feeling component. The following shows the relationships among the Inner Self, our thoughts, and our feelings.

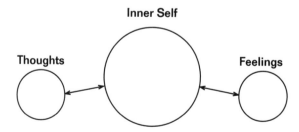

Notice that the connection between the Inner Self and Thoughts and the Inner Self and Feelings is a two-way street. Our thoughts and feelings embed beliefs into the Inner Self. Once those beliefs are in place, they can drive both our thoughts and feelings. This is important to remember as you proceed with redesigning your relationship with money. Any attempts to change our belief system—our thoughts—must incorporate both of these elements. Take some time now to write down the feelings associated with the beliefs you have identified.

As you are constructing your ideal relationship with money, be aware of the feelings that accompany these new beliefs. Your thoughts and feelings must be in alignment. If they're not, your Inner Self will continue holding onto your old beliefs and won't accept the new. For example, you may decide that part of your ideal relationship to money would be the belief: "The money I need to fulfill all my wants flows to me effortlessly." But if you say this statement to yourself and your stomach ties itself into knots, then your feelings and beliefs are not in alignment and your Inner Self won't accept the new belief—no matter how many times you say it.

Often we need to take small steps when redesigning our belief system. Think about your ideal money relationship. How did you respond to that part of the questionnaire? What changes might you make at this point? Write out this ideal relationship as clearly as you can, avoiding vague words like "good" or "a lot" or "very." Try to picture yourself in this ideal state as you write. What steps will you have to go through to get to this place? Rarely can we leap from where we are right now to where we want to be. Indeed, expecting ourselves to make such a leap will probably sabotage the entire effort. Trying to move too fast can overwhelm the psyche and shut down our progress. Remember, you're dealing with a belief system that has been constructed over your lifetime up to this point. Many of those beliefs were instilled in your Inner Self at a very young age.

## Redesigning Your Money Messages

Let's take another look at the previous example of an ideal relationship with money: "The money I need to fulfill all my wants flows to me effortlessly." There may be several messages to be dealt with before this ideal situation can be realized. For example, you may need to develop a stronger sense of what your work is worth. You may need to gain a clearer sense of independence from family messages that no longer serve you in a positive way. You may need to be more comfortable talking about money and learning about how to handle it. These are all steps that need to be taken on the way to developing your ideal relationship with money. They can't be skipped. And each step must have a positive feeling attached to it.

Once you have developed a clear sense of your ideal relationship with money and you have identified the steps involved in getting to that point, you are ready to begin consciously changing the money beliefs currently residing in your Inner Self. We're going to use a technique we introduced you to in Chapter 2.

The first step in this process is to have a clear statement of the new belief. We encourage you to write out the belief statement rather than trying to hold it in your memory. The wording is very important. It should be clear and to the point. Again, don't use vague words like "very" or "good." A belief statement also ought to be phrased in present tense, as if it were already true. The Inner Self operates only on present time. The simpler the statement, the better. It's easier to remember and there is less likelihood of getting off track with fuzzy meanings.

Finally, make certain you understand every word. Diane once used the statement, "I am moving to higher consciousness" to facilitate her efforts at personal development. Unfortunately, all her endeavors stalled just after she began using this statement. No matter how hard she tried, she could not do any activities, like meditating, that were designed to encourage her personal growth. After several days she finally realized what the problem was: Diane is afraid of heights! Her psyche would not allow her to do anything that would move her "higher."

Once you have worked out the statement itself, it's time to connect the feeling with it. To do this, sit quietly and repeat your new belief to yourself. Search your past for a time when you felt the way you want to feel around this concept. Recall those feelings. Let them move through you, anchoring themselves in your body. Firmly connect these feelings with your new belief by saying it over and over as you feel the positive feelings. Now you are ready for the final step, which will embed your new belief into your Inner Self.

Write your belief statement on many note cards. Place them where you will see them throughout the day—on the bathroom mirror, the night table, the refrigerator, the car sun visor and steering wheel, in a drawer you open often, in your wallet. The idea here is to surround yourself with the belief so that you are repeating it to yourself and being reminded of it indirectly. Each time you say it to yourself, breathe deeply and experience the feelings associated with it.

The most powerful way to accomplish this task is to repeat your new belief at times when the old, contradictory belief system is muted. For example, if we believe we are not worthy of making, say, $30 per hour even though other people in our field with comparable experience and education are making that amount, every time we say to ourselves, "I am worthy of earning $30 an hour," our old belief system is going to reject the statement. You can counteract this rejection by slipping your new belief in the back door, so to speak. You can do this any time you have had a shock to your system, such as when you get a paper cut, stub your toe, run into someone as you turn a corner, or when you have to make some quick maneuver with your car to avoid another driver. These sudden jolts cause a mental shift away from the conscious brain and its dominant belief system, and into a more fluid state of consciousness that is wide open to your new statements.

As soon as you experience one of these shocks, begin saying your new belief over and over. Often, the shift only lasts a few seconds. That's fine. You can repeat your statement several times in those seconds, doing some deep breathing to help you recall the feelings attached to it, and go a long way toward embedding that belief into your Inner Self. You may also notice that as you say your new belief to yourself, you will find yourself calming down from the shock. Instead of making certain negative assessments about the driver of the car who just turned in front of you, you can repeat your new belief to yourself, redesigning your Inner Self and calming your jangled nerves at the same time.

These shifts also occur as we are falling asleep and waking up. Anyone in a meditative state is in one of these shifts. So these are good opportunities for making progress toward your ideal money relationship.

## Becoming Comfortable With Your New Inner Self

Going through the process of redesigning your Inner Self to include your ideal relationship with money will probably put you into what we call the amphibian stage of growth. To understand this phenomenon, think about a tadpole and how it might feel about changing into a frog. The contentment of being a tadpole is one day disturbed by the sense that it is going to change, and that this change is inevitable. With this realization comes the sense that the change is both right and disturbing at the same time. Moving into the unknown is often accompanied by a mixture of contradictory feelings. At some point in this growth process, the tadpole ceases to be comfortable being a tadpole but is not yet fully a frog. So the animal goes back and forth, no longer the familiar tadpole but not yet evolved into a frog. This sense of going back and forth is the amphibian stage that we often experience in our own growth—we are no longer comfortable with our old familiar self, but we have not yet moved into what we are to become. Have you ever experienced these sensations as part of your growth?

Several women have talked to us about this dilemma in response to the concept of an ideal relationship with money. For instance, Marilyn, who earns her living in independent sales, said, "I already know it works to use money as a tool. I just can't sustain it. I slip back into worrying I will run out—become destitute." A reentry student told us, "I would love to have complete confidence in the Universe to supply my needs and wants. When things are going well I'm confident. When cash is low—I worry."

Know that this amphibian stage passes. With determination and a willingness to move through a period of discomfort, you will evolve. Using your belief statements as we have described here will result in change for you. Your Inner Self will be different as a result of your efforts. This is why your ideal relationship with money is so important. If you follow the plan we have suggested, you will get exactly what you have said you want. So being clear is vital.

Some of our questionnaire respondents definitely did not want to address the concept of an ideal relationship to money. They wrote that ideally they wouldn't have to deal with money at all! Or they become even more unrealistic hoping that they would win the lottery and not have to worry about earning money. We empathize with these wishes—they underlie a strong motivation behind our writing this book. But the truth is, money is a fact of our lives and only by being in charge of how we want to relate to it will we understand that money can contribute to our strengths as individuals. Then we can put into practice the advice offered to us by investment experts and align ourselves with a workplace that holds similar healthy beliefs.

Think one more time about your ideal relationship with money. Can you see yourself in this relationship? How do you behave toward money, toward yourself and others from this ideal state? What feelings are a part of this state? Do you walk differently in this ideal relationship? What is different about your life? How many of these changes can you begin incorporating into your daily life now? Take a few moments right now to stop reading and move around as if you had already attained your ideal relationship with money. Notice how you hold your head and the rest of your body. Your movements may be more relaxed and fluid than usual. Practice moving with this mind-set often. In the realm of making manifest that which we say we want, there's a lot to be said for acting as if it already exists.

One common theme among women who describe a clear ideal relationship with money revolves around being able to engage in their true work and to have enough money to meet their needs. A therapist told us that her ideal relationship with money meant "that I will always have faith that I will have enough for needs, wants, and pleasures—that I will always believe in my capacity to obtain what I need." Christine, a student, expressed her wish that "I have enough to cover the bills and take some vacations to explore this great world. I do not want to be controlled by how much I make and chasing that endless rainbow."

Finally, Lori summed up what seemed to be the feelings of many women when she said, "I respect its power, but it doesn't take away mine. I acknowledge it as necessary and important, but it does not take top priority in my life. We develop a relationship where we work together (money and I) to make a positive contribution to the planet, specifically to the women and children."

## Helen's Story

We remember Helen as one of our most enthusiastic participants. She was open about her issues and demonstrated a willingness to tackle just about anything. When we talked about the importance of the feeling element when using affirmations, she became very excited.

> I've been using affirmations for several years with mixed results. I was always very careful about choosing the right words, then repeating them over and over throughout the day. Sometimes they worked and sometimes they didn't. I was never really sure what made the difference. Now I know. When I had a strong feeling sense about the affirmation, the change happened fairly quickly. But when I was detached from it—I mean, it would be something that sounded good but I didn't believe it in my gut—I just couldn't make it happen.
>
> I can laugh about this now, but when I first started using affirmations, I decided to see if I could affirm myself into a new Lexus. Never mind that I didn't have the money for one. Every time I would affirm the new car, my stomach would turn because it reminded me of my unhappy financial situation. I understand now what was happening—I was negating the affirmation with my feelings every time I said it. Eventually, I gave up on the Lexus and began using my affirmation energy on other, more important things. With this new information about connecting feelings to the words, I can be even more focused.

When Helen told us she wanted to affirm herself into a higher income, we coached her to think about a time when she felt deserving of more money and comfortable with a raise. We wanted her to fully recall the feelings associated with increased money. Once she could accomplish this, she was ready to work on the wording for her affirmation and tie the two together.

*Chapter Twelve*

# $\mathcal{M}$oney as Energy

No other area of our questionnaire provoked such a wide range of responses as did our request for comments about the spiritual nature of money and money as energy. We were intrigued by the variety of perspectives on these ideas. We examine the spiritual aspects in Chapter 13. Right now, we focus on money as energy.

Concerning money as energy, some women took the perspective that if they have money, they have energy; in other words, they saw money as a generator of their personal energy. Others wrote that money is simply another form of energy. Several women stated that they did not believe there was a connection between money and energy. Still others chose not to react to the statement at all or responded with a question mark. Quite a range.

Throughout this book we've been exploring how our belief system determines how we relate to money. As you have worked through the exercises, clearing out negative beliefs about money, you have been opening yourself to a positive belief system that will help you change your experience with money. We continue with this framework, that our beliefs determine our reality, realizing that on the subject of money as energy, women have widely ranging views.

## Defining Energy

Let's look at what we mean by energy. While this concept may seem abstract at first, energy is actually an integral part of every one of us.

Talking about energy as a real, concrete substance has become easier thanks to the influx from the Orient of healing and martial arts activities founded on understanding human energy systems. Practitioners of such disciplines as yoga, Tai Chi, Qui Kung, acupuncture, and Aikido, to name a few, talk about Chi ("chee") as the basic energy that sustains life in all living things throughout the universe. Quantum physics says essentially the same thing: Energy can neither be created nor destroyed, only changed. We've all heard people say they're "out of energy." What they really mean is that they're tired. People don't literally run out of energy; they lose the ability to allow energy to flow freely, thereby blocking its natural movement. When that happens, they get tired.

For example, suppose you went through the day with a clenched fist. How would you feel? After a short time, your fingers would hurt from being locked into such a firm position. Eventually, you would block out the pain—it would still be there, but you would no longer feel it. Your hand would be useless to you for most hand-related activities. You couldn't use it for writing or picking up anything or even driving a car. Undoubtedly, by the end of the day you would be more tired than usual. Holding your hand in a fist not only blocks energy from flowing the way it naturally would through your hand, but it also takes energy to maintain the tension in your hand. It's a double whammy on your energy.

When the time came to unfold your fist, you would probably have some difficulty at first. You would certainly begin to feel the pain again as you slowly loosened your fingers, wiggling them to get the circulation going. You would become aware that your entire arm was tired from holding it in such an unnatural way. Certainly there are physical implications in keeping your fist clenched for many hours. But there are also problems that arise from the blocked energy. Your natural body state is one of having just enough tension in your muscles to hold you upright and support movement. Your energy is flowing freely in this state. Any tension beyond that begins to block the flow of energy. This is one reason why stress is so exhausting.

Our energy naturally wants to move freely throughout our bodies. When that happens, we feel lively, enthusiastic and invigorated. Here's a simple exercise you can do to increase your awareness of your own energy:

Sit in a comfortable chair with your feet flat on the floor. Focus your attention on your breathing, following your breath in as you inhale, then following your breath out as you exhale. Do that for a few minutes. Let your hands rest on your lap or at your sides, keeping them at least shoulder width apart.

As you inhale, imagine your breath is coming in through the bottoms of your feet. Sometimes people like to use the image of white light or clear water to help make this image more real. As you inhale, pull the breath all the way up to your heart. As you exhale, allow the breath to flow down both arms and out the palms of your hands. Establish an even rhythm of inhaling through the bottoms of your feet, pulling the breath up to your heart, then exhaling the breath down your arms and out your hands. Do this for three to five minutes.

Now raise your hands off your lap with the palms facing each other about shoulder width apart. Keeping up your cycle of breathing and directing your breath, *slowly* bring your palms together. What do you experience as you do this? Play with moving your hands close together, then apart. Maintain the rhythmic breathing as you do this.

You may have any of a number of common experiences with this exercise. Many people feel a tingling in their hands after a few minutes of directing their exhaled breath out the palms. Other people's hands become very hot. These are sensations of your energy moving. When bringing the hands together, most people feel a resistance like a rubber ball or like-poles of a magnet pushing at each other. This, too, is your energy.

If you have no sensations, try again, keeping your hands apart during the initial breathing and giving yourself plenty of time to establish the inhale/exhale cycle. Control any extraneous thoughts. If you do this exercise while planning tonight's dinner menu or worrying about what's happening at work, you will be distracted from your purpose and directing your energy will be difficult if not impossible. So just keep your attention on your breathing.

Keeping your feet on the floor during this exercise keeps you grounded. However, some people prefer to pull the breath/energy in through the tops of their heads, bringing it to the heart then exhaling it down their arms and out their hands. Others like doing both at the same time—inhaling through both the feet and the head. Use whatever way feels right to you.

The purpose of this exercise is to give you a tangible sense of your own energy, to help you realize that energy is a real force in your life.

## Money and Energy

What does the preceding exercise have to do with money? Here's what Ursula, a counselor, said in response to the money as energy statement. "Money is part of the morphogenic field. When I tap into that field my needs have always been met. I have always had access to more than enough money and I know that I will have enough to accomplish what my Source wants me to accomplish."

Another woman observed, "Money often reflects whether a person's energy is open to receive or not." In other words, when we relate to money as energy, we become free to experience it like any other form of energy—free flowing and available when we are open to it.

A movement therapist expressed her concern about the concept of money as energy. She said, "I've heard that money is thought of as energy and I know people who strongly believe that. But from my perspective they are trying to use that belief as a way to have money without earning money." Certainly, this notion can look like a cop-out and we don't doubt that some people who talk about money as energy may use it as an excuse to believe that money will magically come to them. However, we believe this latter view lacks a deep understanding of the nature of energy and money.

Let's look at a slightly different yet parallel concept of how energy manifests in our lives. You have probably heard the saying, "We become what we think about." In other words, at this moment we are each the sum total of all our thoughts up to this time. Why is that? Like everything else, thoughts are forms of energy *and action follows thought.* If we think about something often enough and if desire accompanies that thought, we will take *action* to make the thought a reality. We often don't realize that's what we're doing, but we follow this pattern throughout our lives. If, on the other hand, we lazily think of something—a fantasy here, a wish there—and don't believe we can ever have what we're wishing for, then the negative belief will override the fantasy and we will take no action. Our "action" will be to sabotage the wish. The energy in the fantasy becomes like the clenched fist, blocked and going nowhere.

Relating to money as a form of energy doesn't mean we stop having to work to generate an income. It does mean that our approach to work may change. And certainly our relationship with money will change. We want to keep all energy in our lives flowing naturally. So we will avoid, as much as possible, stressful situations that block energy. We will stay away from toxic people and toxic work conditions that inhibit and drain our energy. We will insist on working in healthy ways that keep our energy in all its forms moving. We will apply the exercises in this book to release negative beliefs about ourselves and money. Each step we take toward a positive relationship with money allows the energy that *is* money to circulate more easily in our lives.

Shirley, a business owner, noted that the idea of money as energy is both "powerful and beneficial." Similarly, a case manager said, "I believe that money is a powerful energy form to be acknowledged and respected and passed on." One woman put it quite simply: "Everything is energy."

We respect the struggle that many women have with this concept. It's very different from what most of us are taught. To see money as part of the natural flow of the universe is to take away much of the meaning attached to it by society. Notions like "Money equals power," "The amount of money an individual has determines that person's worth," and "There is not enough money to go around" all crumble when money is understood to be just another form of energy.

Relating to money as energy gives us a new kind of power in that relationship, too. As we experience the normal flow of energy through our own bodies, we can relate to a natural flow of money through our lives—in as well as out! As we reconceptualize money as energy, thinking about money in a new way, we can find more creative ways to generate money. And we understand that, like any other form of energy, money needs to circulate. Does this mean that we don't save or invest? No. It means that we see ourselves as part of the abundance of energy in the universe and we understand that for it to flow naturally, we must allow that to happen. We must unclench our fist. So we handle money wisely, learning ways we can guide it to generating more for us, and at the same time we understand that if we try to desperately hang on to it with that clenched fist, we will stop the natural energy flow.

Diane recalls a time when her financial situation was extremely delicate. She had a lot of uncertainty about her ability to meet her basic money needs. So every bill became a source of worry and every trip to the grocery store a cause of anxiety. It was easy for her to plug into the fear of lack so dominant in our society and close her fist tightly around what little money she had. But this posture only made things worse.

Realizing that the stress of the situation was interfering with the natural flow of energy, she began to engage in several practices that she still uses today. Any time she paid cash for something, she made certain she handed the bills over with the motto, "In God we trust" facing up. She arranged the currency in her wallet so that she would see this phrase when she reached for a bill. These actions reminded her that she was part of a larger order and that she needed to trust in herself as well as a higher power. They also reminded her that what she released, she would have returned to her. Similarly, when she wrote a check for an expense, she replaced her old anxiety about dwindling funds with the thought, "I am grateful for the money to pay this bill." This helped her relax, loosen her closed mental fist, and allow the energy around money to flow as it is intended.

While her financial situation is now much better, she still engages in these acts as a reminder that money, like all energy, needs to be free to circulate. And that money, like all energy, is abundant. What have you done to help yourself slowly but steadily relax your closed money fist?

While we can have a concrete experience of feeling our energy between the palms of our hands, translating this to a belief about money can be challenging. A parent and homemaker admitted in response to the idea of money as energy, "I understand it intellectually. I can even see it. But . . . ." This shift in belief is aided by reminding ourselves of the ways we experience energy manifesting in our lives. For example, we may finally have achieved something that we had thought about and worked toward for a long time. We're not dismissing the work involved when we say that if we had never had the original thought, the energy form of that achievement, we never would have accomplished it. It took Diane thirteen years to get her first book published. Certainly she worked hard to make that happen. But at the same time, she maintained a clear image of the published book. In other words, she kept the energy around the book moving by thinking of it in its final form.

## Trust

Trust is a critical ingredient in accepting money as energy. Acquiring this ingredient can be challenging because our society does not encourage trust in something that cannot be quantified and measured. The irony of this condition is that trusting in this concept becomes easier each time we demonstrate to ourselves that relating to money as energy results in positive changes. But we have to trust *first* in order to experience the tangible results. We see women struggle with trusting themselves and their unique way of thinking and creating and feeling. Women frequently get messages that we cannot trust our intuition, that our holistic way of thinking and creating is flawed, and that feelings ought to be pushed aside. So we have to learn to trust ourselves in order to thrive and be healthy. Inevitably, when we do trust our intuition, following its guidance, we make healthy decisions. Can you think of examples of this kind of trust in your life?

Likewise, we have to trust that money is no different from any other energy and that, like all other forms of energy, money flows abundantly. Ellen, a woman who gave up a six-figure income to devote herself to writing, her passion, summarized the issue of trust: "I am finally starting to believe and trust that the more I follow my instincts, the more the money for what I need will appear." Similarly, a therapist in private practice illustrated her experience with trust when she told us, "Every time I see my referrals begin to drop and I panic, I seem to unconsciously set up a chain of events that guarantee the downward process will continue. In other words, the more I worry about money, the fewer clients I have. This cycle became apparent to me quite a while back, so I have learned to trust, to believe that my work is important—I will continue. When I release my fears, referrals increase." Diane's and Kay's experiences echo this woman's affirmation.

So what are your thoughts about money as energy? How did you respond to that statement when you completed the questionnaire?

Try this experiment. For the next week or two, turn your bills in your wallet so you can see the ``In God we trust'' motto. Make certain this slogan is facing up when you hand anyone money. If you leave a server's tip on the table, place the bills motto-side up. Also, make a mental note of the saying as you release your hold on the paper. Affirm to yourself that what you are putting out, you will get back. Energy is like that. When you pay bills by check, express your gratitude for having the money to do so.

Practice releasing your energy as you face any negative issues about money. If you feel yourself getting bogged down in destructive thoughts or feelings about money, remember the breathing/energy exercise. Take a few moments to do the exercise, recognizing that money can flow just like your energy and that it will, if you let it. If there have been any exercises in this book that have brought about a stopping of your energy flow, revisit those exercises, doing them this time in conjunction with the breathing exercise.

After giving yourself a reasonable amount of time to make these changes, notice how your relationship to money has changed. You may even want to keep a money journal to track these changes so you can appreciate the progress you have made.

Remember that relating to money as energy is really just applying something that you have been doing all your life in a new direction. So give it time to take hold in your life. Your relationship with money will take on an entirely new dimension from this perspective.

Think about the clenched fist image again. Every time we worry or obsess about money, it's as if we're tightening our grip on what we have. We're reacting out of fear and that stops the natural movement. Perhaps you have relaxed that fist somewhat. Take a look at your genogram again. How would other family members' fists look? How does yours look in comparison? Remember what life was like when your fist was tightly closed. When did you begin to relax and allow money to move more naturally in your life? What are you able to do or have today because of honoring this flow? Celebrate this movement in your life. See that fist relaxing even more. What do you imagine your life will be like at that point? The clearer your images, the easier it will be for you to accept that money is just another energy form.

*Chapter Thirteen*

# $\mathscr{T}$he Spiritual Nature of Money

The idea of money having any spiritual connection may seem improbable to many women. After all, money has generally been viewed as anything *but* spiritual. Most of us are accustomed to relating to money on a mundane, I-need-to-pay-my-bills level. And we have all received messages about the negative, sometimes downright evil, nature of money and the people who have a lot of it. The spiritual realm is usually thought of as being on a very different, much more positive, plane. But just as we can see money as another form of energy, so, too, can we find a spiritual aspect to money.

## Women and Spirituality

One thing many people do when the subject of spirituality comes up is to confuse it with religion. We're not talking about religion here, we're talking about our spiritual Self that gives us our identity and our deep interconnections with all other beings. Historically, we have been severely persecuted for this expression of uniqueness and self-power. It flies in the face of all those messages telling us what we must be and how we must behave. Women's spiritual voice of truth is frightening to those who are invested in maintaining their illusion of power over others.

Women's spirituality expresses itself in many ways and, like other aspects of women's nature, entwines itself throughout our lives. Women don't separate the spiritual from the rest of our lives. We give a voice to our spiritual nature in how we treat all living beings, as well as in how we approach our work and our play. Traditionally women have celebrated and nurtured feminine spirituality in Nature, during solstice and full-moon celebrations, for example. Unfortunately, the rise of patriarchal religion denigrated these celebrations, effectively separating women from our strongest source of spirituality—Mother Nature.

One of the most exciting happenings in recent years is the resurgence of women coming together to nurture each other's spiritual connections. Women have been doing this with Nature-related rituals, group meditations, healing circles, and prayer. We have been focused on our personal growth, nurturing a deep connection with the true Self. And we are constantly integrating this emerging Self, this inherently spiritual being, into our daily lives.

The authors' experience in workshops and private practice tells us that women from all backgrounds, career paths, education, and income levels are engaged in this movement toward spiritual integration. Recently, Diane was asked to give a talk on women's spirituality to a businesswomen's group. The room overflowed with enthusiastic women—reportedly the largest crowd the group had ever had. Women are hungry to know more about their spiritual selves and how to express that Self in all aspects of their lives. Since money pervades just about every part of our lives, why shouldn't it also have a spiritual aspect? As women redefine our role in society, speaking from truthful voices about who we are, shouldn't we redefine money at the same time?

## Money and Spirituality

Let's go back to the questionnaire again. How did you respond to the idea "spiritual nature of money"? Many women in our survey left it blank. Others flatly stated that there is no relationship between the two, while an equal number clearly struggled to find the bond. Then there were those women who understood the connection and articulated it beautifully. So our respondents held many different opinions.

One frequently expressed perspective was that money and spirituality are virtual opposites. Susan, a consultant, said, "I feel most spiritual in nature when money is not an issue." Another woman stated, "We let money come before our spirituality too much of the time. Yes, we need money, but it shouldn't rule us." This concern was expressed by a systems analyst who wrote, "If you don't control it [money], it can become evil." And an art instructor said, "It is a medium for barter, for most of what draws us away from our spiritual growth."

These women are expressing a common concern—that money, because it is "of the world" cannot have a spiritual component, and that, indeed, money is likely to be a barrier to our spirituality. We ask that these beliefs be examined in a larger perspective, one that opens us to the notion that money is simply a tool that can enable us to accomplish our life's purpose. This is the true spiritual aspect of money.

Several women in our survey obviously struggled to come to this belief. Lara, a college student, voiced this difficulty: "I think that money allows people to surround themselves with the resources that they need to survive. However, I think that money can also have an antispiritual nature, too." Actually, people determine whether money will be a barrier to their spirituality or a means to express that spiritual nature. Too often we like to blame money for our attitudes toward it. "Money is the root of all evil" is, as we discussed earlier, a misquote. Yet it is what we all heard growing up. The accurate quote is, "The love of money is the root of all evil." What a vast difference!

## Life's Purpose

Shifting into the belief that money has a spiritual aspect is easier when we look at our life's purpose. What do you believe you are here to do? What is your life's work? What do you most enjoy doing? What jazzes you? Perhaps you might want to make some notes about this that you can refer to later. The answers to these questions usually take some time. Give them some thought before reading on.

For more direction about recognizing your life's purpose, complete the following sentences:

In the past month, I have had the most fun _____

_____.

In the past six months, I have gotten the most satisfaction when I

_____

_____.

In the past year, the most enjoyable and rewarding activity I've been engaged in was _____

_____.

As a child, I especially enjoyed _____

_____.

When I think about doing something that is deeply satisfying, I can see myself _____

_____.

Now read what you have written. What do your responses have in common? Can you see a familiar thread running through them? If your responses seem totally dissimilar, show them to a friend and ask what she can see. Our life's purpose is tied to activities that are both gratifying and enjoyable. Often the skills involved are easy for us, so we may overlook our abilities.

Now complete this sentence:

My life's purpose is _____

_____.

Read your statement out loud so you can hear it. How do you feel about it? Positive, confirming, even joyous feelings mean you are speaking your Truth.

Here are some purpose statements written by workshop participants:

My life's purpose is to teach love to myself and others.

My life's purpose is to live my life in peace and harmony.

My life's purpose is to work with animals.

My life's purpose is being.

When the authors work with someone to help her discover her life's purpose, we look for those events in her life about which she is most enthusiastic. Look at your responses to the previous exercise. Where is your enthusiasm? A great word, "enthusiasm." It comes from the Greek *entheos* that means inspired or with god. So whatever excites us in our lives gives us significant clues about our purpose. As people become clearer about their purpose, they generally move into a more spiritual aspect. That is, they see their life from a broader and deeper perspective than the usual daily routine. This view is frequently aligned with our spiritual nature.

If people do have a life's purpose—and we believe that everyone does—then it is reasonable to expect that the universe's abundance must be available to support that purpose. In other words, it makes no sense to believe we all have a life purpose and then not believe that the universe would provide for the fulfillment of that purpose. Are we saying that the universe wants everyone to have a million dollars? No. Most of us don't need that much money to live a rewarding life.

Too often artificial wants, generally created by advertising and/ or family fears, interfere with our sense of fulfillment. We have worked with many people who use their financial resources to maintain a lifestyle rather than to help them fulfill their life's purpose.

And they wonder why they are frustrated! This situation isn't money's fault; it's the result of how people conceptualize and use money.

We wonder how many businesses have had something similar happen. An individual has a vision for a business and proceeds to fulfill that vision. Generally, a vision becomes a reality because it is part of a person's life purpose, whether that individual realizes it or not. So an entrepreneur builds an organization initially from a drive to fulfill his or her purpose. The business is the vehicle for that fulfillment and the money it generates sustains the entire process. Too often, however, the incentive to make money just for the sake of making money takes over. When that happens, the vision is lost and the joy is gone. The spiritual connection disintegrates.

Knowing ourselves at the spiritual level means we understand the difference between our needs and our wants. It means we can walk away from that which does not spiritually satisfy us and embrace the ideas, activities, and relationships that help us fulfill our soul needs. This focus on fulfilling ourselves spiritually automatically causes everything in our lives to expand—our creativity, energy, joy, even money.

## Spirituality, Money, and Reality

When we discuss with a group the notion of a spiritual aspect of money, we are frequently asked about how this concept fits with the more commonly accepted "reality" of money that says, "More is better." Our groups also want to know how it fits with a society in which salary inequities abound. What about CEOs who make seven-figure salaries and are further rewarded with additional money when they lay people off? Where's the spirituality in that? At first glance, there doesn't appear to be any. But how do we really know? In the larger scheme of things, perhaps these things happen in order to bring to light the gross inequities in our economic system. We're not justifying these corporate behaviors, just suggesting there might be a different way of looking at them.

What is most important in this discussion is for each individual to understand money's spiritual aspect as it relates to her personally. Too often when we try to understand money from a spiritual perspective, we are looking through a lens colored and distorted by negative messages. In other words, we try to see the new by looking through the old. This perspective doesn't work. We need to look at money anew, seeing it as a tool to support our life's purpose. From this vantage point, we can then look differently at how people manifest money in their lives. Instead of attempting to view the spiritual by looking from a worldly perspective, we are looking at the worldly through the spiritual. From this vista, the view is entirely changed. And it matters less what others do or don't do with money and more what our beliefs are about money.

Here's what some women have had to say about this view. Regarding the spiritual nature of money, one woman said, "It's about flowing, life's purpose, service, and trusting God." Lori told us, "The issues I deal with daily, many of which are spiritual in nature, show up in every area of my life. I am given many opportunities to learn about myself and to work through my fears. Money is one of many teaching tools for me as I learn to walk through Fear. . . . I believe abundance affirmations can also be a valuable tool as I co-create [with God] the money I need."

A former sales manager expressed the challenge in accepting this belief when she wrote, "I do believe that if you follow your instincts, the universe will provide—but sometimes it's really hard to let go and just believe that."

## New Possibilities

In accepting that money has a spiritual component, we call into question how society views money. All our messages about how we should relate to money get tossed into the air. New possibilities abound.

The spiritual gives meaning to our lives. And it emerges from the depths of our being to be manifested in a simple act of kindness, in saying no to that which might harm us, in large and small ways every day. When we connect with our spiritual nature, we move out of our "little local self," the worrier who buys into negative beliefs about money, and into resonance with all-that-is. Our spiritual Self is a larger self who understands the interconnection among all beings and who understands that what we put out, we get back. It taps into an unlimited supply of energy and accepts that the universe provides what we need.

## Coping With Fear

Unfortunately, much of our thinking, and we're including individual and corporate here, is still dominated by fear of poverty, by a belief in lack. This can drive greed, the fear that "I might not get mine, so I better grab all I can." Fear always separates us from our spirituality. Facing our fears by knowing our own Truth moves us back into connection with our spiritual Self. From this place we can remind ourselves of a larger order that transcends fear-based beliefs. Look over the exercises you've done so far in this book. What fears do you have about money? Review your responses to the questionnaire for fear-based beliefs. People are often uncomfortable when facing fears, so a feeling of discomfort can be a sign that you are on the right track. Now try this exercise:

Divide a sheet of paper into two columns. Label the left column **Money Fears** and label the right, **The Truth**. In the Money Fears column, list as many fears as you are aware of. Remember that sometimes fears disguise themselves. For example, fear of lack can manifest itself in hoarding behaviors, in reluctance to enjoy what money can buy, even in greed. Make some notes about how your fears translate themselves into behavior. Write down how you feel when you are caught in the fear. Note any sensation of familiarity surrounding the fear.

Next, for each fear, recall who first gave you the fear. Our beliefs about money are all manufactured. Now is the time to discover whose fears you have been carrying in your belief system. In The Truth column, note whose voice you hear behind the fear. (Consulting your genogram might be helpful at this point.)

Then write out a positive belief that you want to replace the fear, one that is appropriate for you now. Be simple, direct, and positive in your language. For example, the fear of becoming a bag lady might be replaced with the truthful statement, "I am competent in handling my finances" or "I generate enough money to meet my needs." Remember to be careful with the words you choose—they can be powerful.

Looking at your new truthful statement, allow an appropriate positive emotion to arise. How do you want to feel instead of fearful? Write down that feeling, tying it to the statement.

Imagine how your behavior would change if you acted as if the new statement were true. What would you do to stay aligned with your Truth? How would your relationship to money change? Think about the little changes as well as the larger ones. Make some notes about what these positive behaviors would be.

Keep this list handy so you can add to it. Let it remind you of what you want your beliefs to be and how you want to feel and act as you assume an increasingly powerful relationship with money. When you catch yourself engaging in fear-based behaviors or thinking fearful thoughts, go to your list so you can see your Truth. Repeat the statement out loud, allowing yourself to feel the charge of positive emotions connected with your Truth. With persistence and vigilance, you can face your fears and, exposing them to your Truth, rid yourself of outdated beliefs that keep you from enjoying a healthy relationship with money.

Another technique that is helpful in moving us out of our fears is the energy-generating exercise given in Chapter 12. Using that exercise can help keep us attuned to our spiritual Self because it moves us out of our worrier self. And it reminds us that abundance is basic in the universe.

## Accepting Abundance

We frequently hear about the top ten billionaires in the world, or the wealthiest sports figures, or the world's richest women. The total wealth of these few people is staggering. People react to this information with wide-ranging emotions—jealousy, disgust, anger, indifference. Regardless of our reaction to so much wealth concentrated in the hands of so few, one point remains: Adequate monetary wealth *does* exist on this planet. The problem is that it is held by very few people. The abundance is tied up; it's not flowing. Are we advocating that all money be forcefully redistributed? No, we are simply encouraging a larger view of money, a view that money is plentiful. Opening our beliefs about money opens us spiritually to accept more abundance into our lives.

Certainly there are many forms of abundance, including intangibles such as happiness, satisfaction, or love. These are undeniably important. But it's often easier to think of love as being abundant than it is money, even though money is more tangible. Sometimes people tell us lots of reasons why they struggle with this idea. Most of these reasons usually arise from family and societal messages and from an individual's devotion to maintaining the correctness of these beliefs.

We've explored all this in previous chapters and by now you have taken a hard look at your messages. Clearing out unwanted, untrue beliefs is important because they are likely to be at the root of many dissatisfactions about money. If we believe adequate money exists to meet everyone's spiritual needs, there's no reason why we can't have the amount of money we need. We won't be depriving anyone else of money since there's enough for everyone. Fear of being greedy or selfish, two messages that often inhibit women in attaining more money, evaporate when money is seen as part of the abundant nature of the universe.

We want to be clear about another point. Sometimes people talk about abundance, then simply expect a lot of money to appear. This sort of "All things come to those who wait" mentality can be an excuse for not expressing one's purpose. Simply knowing our life's purpose doesn't automatically mean we will live it. We will be miserable if we don't, but we do have a choice. We may falsely believe that we would be safer not pursuing our purpose, because living that purpose often means change and risk. So we maintain the status quo, even when it is unhealthy for us. The authors have seen people do the same thing with the notion of adequate resources available to support one's purpose. Afraid to take a risk, to move out of their safe place, they wait for everything to come to them. Or they surround themselves with people holding similar opinions. They may even work for an organization that reinforces their negative beliefs. Their stagnation is supported. True change in belief is accompanied by a change in action.

Accepting that abundant financial resources exist right now for you to realize your life's purpose means clearing out old, irrelevant messages, which takes work. It means trying out new behaviors, taking risks. We have seen people who espouse a spiritual aspect of money and who then express this belief through inaction. Granted, this is safe, but is that truly the point?

When the issue of action versus inaction comes up, Diane is reminded of a former client, an artist who decided that she wanted a gallery to approach her to display her work. The commonly held belief in the art world is that the artist must beat down the doors of many galleries and suffer much rejection before ever being seriously considered. This woman realized the improbability of her goal, but stayed with her vision. In the meantime, she painted, developing her skill and her courage to express on canvas ever-deeper levels of herself. She gave talks on her by now well-developed expertise. Over time, she created paintings with universal themes that reached deep into the human psyche. She also entered a few select shows, keeping her growing body of work before the public eye. Eventually, she was approached by a prestigious gallery. So while she "waited," she worked very hard, believing in her vision.

Accepting the spiritual aspect of money is like the artist's experience. Even when the idea runs contrary to commonly accepted belief, it can still be true for the individual. Believing in financial abundance doesn't mean that what you want will automatically come to you. It does mean that in living out your life's purpose, in living with enthusiasm, you will have dissolved the blocks that have previously been inhibiting you. In freeing up the energy bound in negative, untrue beliefs, we let loose tremendous energy for being creative. And we overthrow an archaic belief system about money that never supported fulfilling our spiritual nature. Now we are redefining money on *our* terms, creating an energy form that serves our spiritual selves the way we want it to.

## Kerri's Story

When we first talked about money existing to support my purpose, I quickly agreed. I mean, it sounded right. But as time went on, I began to realize that I didn't really understand the connection between money and spirituality. I think too many of my old ideas about money got in the way. So I just kept plugging away at them, getting rid of as many unhealthy beliefs as I could.

At the same time, I kept thinking about the spiritual aspect of money and what that might mean for me. I kept affirming that money exists to support me in pursuit of my purpose. I always thought I had a pretty good idea of why I'm here but I never realized that money is here so I can fulfill my purpose. Once I truly allowed myself to believe this, I could feel myself moving steadily away from my old negative beliefs and toward a positive belief system.

I knew I had made major progress one day when I was at a budget meeting. I just sat back and listened to all the destructive money beliefs being thrown around that table. I kept thinking that our company earns money to fulfill its purpose, just like each of us does. I started to explain this idea to my co-workers, but I could see it was beyond them. So now I bring up the subject when it's appropriate with one person at a time.

I don't care whether or not anyone else agrees with me at work; I know what a difference this perspective has made for me. I'm relaxed about money and I feel as if I have a healthy relationship with it for the first time in my life.

## Chapter Fourteen

# *M*oney Messages in the Workplace

Just as each of us has our set of money messages, so, too, do the companies and organizations we work for. As you are clearing out your unwanted messages and redefining money, begin looking at the beliefs about money that are embedded in your workplace. What are the underlying convictions held by the organization you work for? What messages do you hear about abundance and scarcity, about the distribution of money both within the organization and to the outside, about the true purpose for money within the company? Where do these messages come from? Who perpetuates the company's belief system about money?

And consider the possibly most important question, What are the similarities between the money beliefs held in your workplace and those you hold? In the whole process of reevaluating your relationship with money and moving into a healthier position, examining how your workplace reinforces your old belief system is very important. We have been leading you through a challenging process of change resulting in your being able to completely redefine money on your own terms. You have come to the place where you are relating to money in a new, much more healthy way. From this perspective, you may begin to see other people's relationships with money in a new way. Now we want to focus on the money attitudes that predominate in your workplace.

As you have probably observed during this process of change, one of the aspects of human nature that makes change so challenging is that most people want to be comfortable. Hence, we generally try to keep ourselves in familiar situations and to surround ourselves with familiar people. For example, people commonly reconstruct their family of origin when they marry and create their own family. We've all heard the notion that men marry a woman who is like their mother and women marry a man who is like their father. Certainly there are exceptions to this, but the point is that we naturally want to surround ourselves with the comfortable and the familiar. But in going through change, we must put ourselves into uncomfortable, unfamiliar situations. We grow and change to the degree that we can tolerate the accompanying discomfort. We know we've succeeded in changing once we become comfortable with new behaviors and situations.

You've probably already encountered this dynamic in going through this book. Now as you move into a new, healthier relationship with money, the unhealthy ways that people have of relating to money may become more noticeable to you. This is especially true in close relationships. And one of your closest relationships is the one you have with your employer. If you haven't already begun to examine the money messages inherent in your workplace, now is the time to do so.

## Corporate Values and Personal Values

It would be natural to be drawn into an organization that has essentially the same beliefs about money that you do. A belief that money exists primarily to support people in the pursuit of an enjoyable living would draw you into a workplace that encourages people to do their best work and to have fun with it. If you have believed that money is scarce, you would probably feel comfortable working in an atmosphere that supported that belief. Annette, a participant in one of our workshops, shared the following story as an example of how her old beliefs were played out in the workplace:

> Looking back, I can see how a job I once had illustrates being trapped by old messages. I grew up in a home where there was never enough. There were five children and our alcoholic father was frequently out of work. Consequently, everything seemed to be rationed—food, paper goods, everything. Money never seemed to go very far and we had to be very thrifty. Talk about scarcity—that's how I lived my early years. After I graduated, I took a position in the student service department of a large university. My first boss would have made Ebenezer Scrooge look generous. He acted like the college's money came out of his pocket. Although taking classes at a reduced tuition rate was part of our employee benefit package, the boss made sure that if we did so during the daylight hours, we made up every minute we were away from our desks. It seems really silly to think about it now, but we had to tally up our missed coffee breaks and lunch hours to accumulate enough time to take classes. What made it even more demeaning was that the classes I was taking weren't just for fun, they improved my workplace skills! It was so easy for me to accept this demand even when it seemed humiliating.
>
> That pattern of having to account for every penny was one I knew well from my childhood. After I learned about transferring past messages into the workplace, I realized that I had fallen into the trap of continuing to live out that message of extreme thrift. I now work for a company that sees continuing training as a benefit to both the employer and employee.

What dominant money beliefs have you identified for yourself up to this point? Do you hear similar messages around work? What do these beliefs mean to how you can do your work? Now that you are clearing out old, unhealthy messages and embracing a positive relationship with money, how will that change your relationship to your workplace?

Stop at this point and think about these questions. Make some notes of your responses. These will give you a framework for the rest of this chapter.

During the eighties, American business drastically cut money invested in research and development. Just like individuals who don't want to plan for their financial future, cutting out R&D is withdrawing support for the company's future. Satisfying immediate needs without providing for development of tomorrow's products is as short-sighted as spending your "extra" money at the end of the month so you won't have to learn about investing. The dynamic is essentially the same. If I spend it somewhere else, I don't have to plan, research, develop, and take risks. How many people are unconsciously drawn into companies with this type of philosophy because they hold the same belief about their own finances?

One theme that seems to have been dominant among American businesses since the 1980s is that "money is tight." Does your organization operate unyder this belief system? Do you? Many of us have been a part of a company that preached this belief most of the year only to have various departments scramble to spend as the fiscal year came to a close. This spending would occur either because the money had to be spent or it would be taken away, or because that department would not be re-funded to an equal or greater amount if it didn't spend its budget for the current fiscal year. Jana told us about her experience with this phenomenon:

> Becoming aware of my money messages helped me see some things I had been oblivious to before. I clicked onto how stressful the ''money is tight but spend it quick'' philosophy was for me when I came to work near the end

of June and found our workspace all torn up. Our managers had made a last-minute decision to have new carpeting installed before the fiscal year ended. We had not been able to get adequate supplies all year and now this frenzy of spending before the year was up seemed really contra-dictory. This was our busiest time in terms of our level of cus-tomer service, but we were told the carpeting couldn't be done when the office was closed. The installers would charge time and a half if they had to work on weekends! In the past I would have shrugged off this kind of illogic but now it occurred to me that it was time to polish up my re-sume and start looking for a company that was a better fit for me.

Businesses have their conflicting messages about money just like in-dividuals do.

Another aspect to examine in looking for similarities between your attitudes toward money and those of your employer is the for-profit or not-for-profit purpose of an organization. Traditionally, the private sector has been dominated by money attitudes such as more is better; bigger is better; people are paid according to their worth in the company; people work hard for their money. Nonprofits have also had their notions about money, such as employees are driven by their service to others, not by money; people are not paid what their work is worth but, rather, by a standard that applies to everyone; working purely for money is demeaning. The for-profit sector often looks down on the public sector, embracing stereotypes such as people working "at the public trough" are lazy; people in the nonprofits can't make it in the more challenging world of for-profits. Conversely, the nonprofit sector can often be heard to reinforce stereotypes such as people working in the private sector are interested only in money; the private sector is hard-hearted and doesn't care about people.

Regardless of where you find yourself employed, it's important to eliminate any of these stereotypes you may be carrying. After a thorough personal evaluation, you may find yourself more suited to working in a different type of business, moving, say, from the public to the private sector, or vice versa. Stereotypes will only make your transition more difficult. The truth is, both sectors have their money-motivated people and their more altruistic employees. Both share inept as well as outstanding managers. Lazy and industrious employees can be found everywhere. Neither the public nor the private sector has a monopoly on virtue or competence. Letting go of such stereotypes helps us clear our vision so we can focus on what is truly important—our own personal and professional growth.

Working for a profit-making business doesn't necessarily mean you have to be motivated by money. What you need to be aware of are the attitudes toward money that dominate within the profit-making structure. Certainly, the private sector is in business to make money. How companies go about reaching that goal—their service to customers and to employees—makes all the difference. And the nonprofit sector must have money to operate, even if finances are not the bottom line. But many people who are drawn to working in the nonprofit environment have difficulty when the subject of generating money comes up. And this challenge is reinforced by the money attitudes that dominate. For example, asking for a raise in the public sector is generally fruitless and is sometimes met with ridicule. Yet we know that merit raises motivate people. They tell employees that their work is valuable and is noticed. This kind of validation is usually lacking in the nonprofit sector. The for-profit sector, however, expects people to ask for what their skills are worth. So the expectations about money are very different in these two work environments. Knowing your money value system is important so that you can situate yourself in the atmosphere that serves you better.

Now that you are much clearer about your money messages and committed to developing a healthy relationship with money, you may need to reevaluate how appropriate your choice of employer has been. For example, we have seen enough annual financial plans to know that many companies make impossible demands on their sales staff to produce ever-greater sales, even if the current year's goals haven't been met because those objectives were too high! We know of one consulting firm that set extremely high goals for its staff one year. The consultants pulled together and worked even harder than usual to meet the objectives. And they did it! Much to everyone's surprise. They rightly expected to be rewarded. While bonuses were distributed, upper management set even higher goals for the next year. The exhausted staff was demoralized and the office was riddled with resignations in the following months.

Still, we wonder about what kinds of personal money messages are carried by people who allow themselves to get caught up in trying to meet what they know is an impossible goal. While the company's philosophy is reflected in this type of approach to business, so is the belief system of the individuals involved. The company's demands are reflecting the employee's own inner demands. In the same way we accepted our unconscious money messages without checking to see that they fit who we are today, we may have done likewise with our organization's messages. Now is the time to review and rewrite as appropriate.

To help identify your organization's beliefs about money, try completing these sentences:

My employer uses money to _____
_____.

My boss seems to believe money is _____
_____.

My coworkers seem to believe money is _____
_____.

The phrase I hear most often around my workplace is ``Money is _
_____.

This phrase does/doesn't match my belief system. The phrase I use most often about money is _____

_____.

When discussions about money come up at work, I feel _____

_____.


## Maintaining Loyalty

Just as individuals will maintain beliefs derived from their family in an unconscious attempt to be loyal to the family, so, too, will organizations play out corporate family beliefs. Departing from long-held ideas about anything, especially money, can inspire fear and anxiety about the unknown. If I change my beliefs about money, I will also be changing my behavior not only about money but also in the marketplace. An organization going through change experiences the same concerns. If the CEO adopts the corporate belief that money is abundant, will managers overspend their budgets? Will employees demand ever-higher raises that the company might not be able to afford? What happens to the abundance belief when the economy slows? And how do employees who have bought into the scarcity mentality make the change?

The problem with an organization clinging to an outmoded, unhealthy relationship with money is the damage that it causes. Fear stifles growth. Maintaining loyalty to an inappropriate belief system brings about corporate sclerosis wherein flexibility is gone. Responding to a changing marketplace becomes increasingly difficult. As with individuals who behave in accordance with their beliefs, making certain their reality matches their ideas, so do organizations behave in line with their beliefs. If a company sees itself to be growing, dynamic, and creative, then its employees will behave accordingly. But if an organization believes it must be cautious, not allowing for risk-taking, then its employees will behave to support those beliefs. And these respective attitudes will be reflected in the corporate bottom line. When a nonprofit organization becomes sclerotic, service to clients suffers while fear spreads among employees.

People know when the organizations they are working for aren't keeping up with economic trends. Instead of embracing change with the support of the entire organization, individuals realize, consciously and unconsciously, that the company isn't keeping up. They become fearful of losing their jobs and fearful of change. When fear dominates within an organization, growth stops. At the same time, we have to remember that people are drawn to a company because of an unconscious attraction to its value system. The beliefs that a company is making come true are held by individuals within the organization as well.

## Orchestrating Change

So what happens once you begin changing your beliefs about money? With regard to your workplace, some changes are likely to occur. The most obvious change is that you may decide you need to move to another organization with a belief system about money more in alignment with your own. The realization that such a move is necessary often begins with a vague feeling of not fitting in. This sensation generally begins slowly. It's like putting on a pair of old shoes and expecting them to be comfortable and, to your surprise, they don't feel right. You may keep wearing them, hoping that the old comfort will return. But it never does. Something has changed. In this case what has changed is your relationship to money. Eventually you realize your discomfort in your old workplace comes from a conflict in beliefs around money.

Connie, an apartment manager, told of her decision to change employers:

I realized how tired I was of working for an employer for whom money was always the bottom line. I was trying to run a really nice apartment complex, which meant I sometimes needed to evict people who were loud, consistently made trouble, or, worse still, used drugs. The owners were interested only in keeping spaces rented and didn't care what was going on or how bad the complex was for the good tenants. I was always having to explain my decisions not to rent to just anyone who applied, or to justify having an empty apartment when I asked a bad tenant to leave. The owner didn't seem to understand that while it took time to find responsible renters, once I did, they would stay because the complex would be safe and well run. I know I'm a good manager and I don't need someone looking over my shoulder, questioning my decisions solely on the basis of money. That kind of shortsighted management philosophy was not for me. I found another place that was a much better match with my values and I'm happy I made the change.

After you've decided to move to a different company, research to find out what prospective new employers believe as far as money is concerned. The annual report is a good way to start your investigation. Search out newspaper, magazine, and journal articles, especially those that address managerial attitudes and philosophies. Talk to current employees about the kinds of money messages the company holds. You are not likely to find a perfect match, but you can find organizations that have basically healthy attitudes toward money and its function. You will find it easier to maintain your new, healthy relationship with money when you work for a company that has similar attitudes.

Not everyone wants to find another job. Many people find their work satisfying but have trouble reconciling their newly held beliefs with the old money notions held by the company they work for. Unless you are the CEO or CFO, you probably won't be able to significantly change the money beliefs held corporate wide. Trying to change those beliefs is like attempting to change another person's behavior—it's generally doomed and likely to result only in your extreme frustration. At the same time, we don't want to underestimate the influence you may have. Carefully examine your goal in this regard. You want to preserve your new, healthy relationship with money and share that perspective with others who will listen. Having the goal of changing the corporate culture about money is misguided at best.

That said, suppose you do want to try to influence the perceptions of money in your workplace. Your level of authority within the organization will make a difference here. A department head generally has much more influence throughout the department than does a management trainee or secretary. (Although we would never underestimate the power of an effective secretary!) Regardless of where you find yourself within the corporate structure, you can maintain your uniquely healthy relationship with money in spite of your organization's unhealthy relationship.

Be on the alert to hearing statements about money that contradict your own beliefs. Affirm to yourself when someone voices a negative view of money that that person is entitled to his or her views just as you are certain of your own. In situations where you need to make a comment regarding money, a good way to present an alternate view is to acknowledge the unhealthy attitude by simply stating, "That's one way of looking at this situation. Now I would like to propose a different view." At this point, you can suggest an example of what the circumstance might be like if everyone held a healthier view of money. Describe what the department budget might look like if money were abundant instead of "tight." Often, the budget itself doesn't look significantly different. What changes is the attitude toward using that budget. Or describe what the annual financial plan goals might be if they were developed with full input from the people who had to achieve those goals. Describe what type of workplace everyone would have if making money were a way to stimulate healthy growth in employees as well as the company. "Productive" is the concept that dominates in this last picture.

Changing attitudes takes time. You may never be able to effect much change within your organization. Choosing to stay within a company that holds very different views of money from yours means that you will have to stay firm with your own beliefs and not tie yourself into the company's ideas. You can work within a set budget, for example, without embracing the belief that "money is tight." Be careful what you say to yourself when you have to deal with the budget or develop part of the annual financial plan. Reaffirm your own beliefs about the energy and spiritual aspects of money and let the organizational beliefs be. Think of them as so much refuse. You probably wouldn't pick up orange peels and coffee grounds and other garbage off the street to carry around with you, so don't be tempted to pick up unhealthy beliefs. You can have your healthy relationship with money both at work and at home.

Too often money seems tied to the belief that it is the only indicator of corporate success. Then it becomes a weapon to hold over people and, occasionally, to reward them with. When money is reconceptualized and viewed as a tool to enable the organization to achieve appropriate growth and to acknowledge the efforts of employees who make that growth occur, then the energy around money is freed to flow naturally.

An organization that understands the spiritual nature of money recognizes that it has a purpose that rarely involves making money. The energy of an organization exists for some reason beyond the bottom line. At the same time, the organization realizes it needs to make a profit to stay in business. Sometimes companies know their true purpose and have stated it in their mission statements. Often, however, they miss the point of their own existence. When an organization does realize its mission, it then becomes free to fulfill that purpose in as many ways as it can support. In our economic system, this fulfillment takes money. So many companies have come to believe that they exist to make money. This belief limits an organization just as it does an individual. Once a company embraces the notion that the money it generates exists so that the company can provide a satisfying work environment where people earn a livable wage and so investors can make money to support them in their purpose, the entire culture is changed.

Workers are drawn to the organization because of a similarity in purpose. Individuals stop trying to protect their territory and become more inclusive of others. A true team spirit dominates because virtually everyone is committed to making the company a success. That success means employees can pursue their purpose, which may or may not be tied to the company's purpose. Whether these two are related is irrelevant because what is important is the knowledge that everyone understands the spiritual nature of money.

Once employees embrace a healthy attitude toward money, the entire organization moves forward. The corporate culture has changed.

## Charlotte's Story

I began my career in advertising with my first job after college. It wasn't my dream job, but it gave me experience. I continued to move on and up, enjoying my successes. But somehow, deep down, I never felt as if I belonged. I got along with my co-workers and did well, but I always felt slightly out of step. Finally, I began to realize that what was important to my employer wasn't especially important to me. Mostly I had problems with how the company went about doing business. Upper management pushed great service to customers but treated employees lousy. Everything became very clear to me one year when annual raises were disbursed. Everyone knew that the big bosses got double-digit raises. None of the rest of us did. I couldn't reconcile this action with the repeated statements about how we had to operate on tight budgets.

That's what motivated me to start looking hard at my money messages. Eventually I got to the place where I couldn't stay with that company. I went to work for another agency but soon found similar negative beliefs around money. I can see now that everything was pushing me to form my own ad agency. It was scary at first, but I realized that I could determine how my company viewed and dealt with money. I've made a concerted effort to infuse my organization with positive beliefs about money and to hire other people who also share these ideas. I've made a commitment to building a different kind of company. I realize that I have to stay healthy in how I relate to money if I want my company to also be healthy, so I have to keep on my toes about my money issues. I'm not a hundred percent where I want to be yet, but I'm developing a good place for people to work.

## Chapter Fifteen

# *W*orking for More Than Money

We would like you to pause and take a moment to congratulate yourself for having come so far on this journey of reconsidering, revising, and reworking your messages about that highly emotional issue—money. This has been no small task, as you now know. Let the impact of what you have accomplished so far sweep through your consciousness. Allow yourself to bask in a feeling of having worked hard and faced down your fears. You may not be exactly where you want to be yet, but allow yourself to rejoice in how far you have come. Feel that new sense of increased personal power as you ready yourself for the next steps.

Having developed a healthier relationship with money, you can move on to yet another aspect of this journey, that of looking at how your work life fits into this new context. In the process of eliminating your old fears and undesirable beliefs about money, your value system has probably changed. Often, people whose primary motivation for working came from the paycheck experience a shift. Now, their drive for working is derived from wanting to fulfill a unique part of themselves. Work becomes a means of self-expression. It takes on a new place in people's lives, moving into balance with other elements important to a happy life, like family, friends, and recreation.

During the five years that Diane worked with laid-off workers, she saw this shift happen repeatedly. Most of her clients were over forty-five and many had devoted themselves to their careers and the companies that employed them. Being laid off was usually a traumatic event that precipitated a close examination of one's money issues. Time and time again these people came to the realization that their emphasis on external rewards had left them feeling hollow and unfulfilled.

With renewed vigor, they undertook an exploration into their Inner Selves, embracing their true Selves and nurturing its emergence. But they still needed to work. So they set out to find a vocation that was aligned with who they were as distinctive individuals. Fed up with putting up with a negative work situation—being laid off let them know there was no reward for tolerating the intolerable—they went in search of healthy workplaces that would bring out the best in them. While money still played a role in this search, it did not have the power it once had in their lives.

When money becomes a tool to help us achieve our life's purpose, we're free to move into a whole new relationship with work. We want to examine six major areas involved in this new, higher level of work consciousness: achieving clarity, finding a joyful workplace, finding coworkers you respect, finding work that fits your money values, understanding your motivation to work, and enhancing your self-esteem through work.

## Achieving Clarity in Your Work Life

You may have already noticed that your new clarity with money issues brings a clearer vision in other areas of your life as well. As you grow in the knowledge of the place money can have in helping you achieve your life's purpose, you become free to take a fresh look at your reasons for working. You focus less on working only to make money and more on balancing other areas of your life. Are we saying that you should not consider money as a factor in your choice of careers? Of course not. What we are saying is that one of the benefits of a clear vision is the freedom to make new choices. Choosing to have your work life enhance your emotional well-being means you seek employment that is soul satisfying as well as financially rewarding.

Dale Dauten, an entrepreneur, speaker, and author, tells of giving speeches on this topic to business groups.[1] When he talks about finding meaning in work, he reports seeing some audience members' eyes glaze over. He knows these are employees who have given up on finding any joy in their work lives; he terms them "the living dead." His charge to employees to find fulfilling work is based on two facts as he sees them: "There are joyful work environments and dreary ones," and, "Ultimately, you become your coworkers."

To assist in the process of finding clarity in your work life, we want to take a closer look at finding joy in the workplace, becoming your coworkers, finding work that fits your money values, and understanding your motivation. We believe in having work that fulfills and gratifies you. Work ought to bring out the best in us. Thus, we will encourage you to make whatever changes are necessary to bring yourself into this kind of work. Here are some points for you to consider as you assess your work life.


## Finding a Joyful Work Environment

What makes a joyful work environment? According to the authors of *Do What You Are,* an important part of finding satisfying work is knowing what to look for.[2] You know you are in the ideal job when you:

- Look forward to going to work.
- Feel energized (most of the time) by what you do.
- Feel your contribution is respected and appreciated.
- Feel proud when describing your work to others.

- Enjoy and respect the people you work with.
- Feel optimistic about the future.

This list certainly sounds like a prescription for a joyful work environment. How many of these elements do you feel daily? We would also add two more items to this list:

- The belief that a joyful work environment is possible
- The knowledge that you deserve to enjoy your work

We have found that many employees have become so burned out and cynical that they no longer believe in the possibility of happiness in the workplace. If this pessimism fits you, we suggest you take some time to review your new beliefs about money. Let them help you focus on what you need to be happy on the job. Your new money attitudes can give you the courage to take a hard look at your place of employment. As you are taking control of your financial life, control of your work life becomes easier. You've already established the precedent of taking care of yourself in a healthy, growth-producing way, so this next step fits in with your new way of thinking.

Ask yourself, "What would I place on my list of characteristics of an ideal job?" Jot down everything that comes to mind without worrying at this point about whether or not it's possible to get them. Work as rapidly as you can—speed will keep you from editing your list. You can do that later. List all the characteristics that come to mind here:

_____

_____

_____

Now go back over your list. Is there anything else you need to add to make this picture fit you? Rate the characteristics you have listed with a 1, 2, or 3. A rating of 3 means this item is absolutely essential, a 2 means it is important, while a 1 denotes a quality that would be nice to have but is not critical to your happiness on the job. What should emerge as you do this exercise is a picture of your ideal job. Now go back one more time and assess how your current job matches up with your ideal job. Is anything missing in your current work? Are there any changes you need to make?

Sometimes when we do the preceding exercise, people automatically feel as if they have to completely change their work situation. While that is true for some people, we have observed that many times an attitude shift on the part of the individual is all that is needed to turn an uncomfortable job into a happier one. Regardless of the action that is appropriate for you, realize what you can change and what is beyond your control. Others' attitudes are out of your control. Your reaction to them, however, is completely within your control. Moving into your ideal work situation will probably be a journey of many steps.

## Finding Coworkers You Respect and Enjoy

The concept that ultimately we can become our coworkers may initially strike some people as odd. You may ask, how can this be and how does it happen? If you stop to think about this phenomenon, you may discover that you have experienced this dynamic without really understanding it for what it was. Have you ever gone into an establishment and found all the employees to be upbeat and smiling? You probably thought to yourself as you walked out, "I'm glad I came in here. What a great place." And you probably did more business with that establishment. You are responding to the emotional climate of that particular workplace. Being positive and enjoying work are contagious. Just as parents set an emotional climate for a family, so your coworkers have the power to set the emotional climate for the workplace. If your coworkers are optimistic and upbeat, this is the atmosphere you will probably experience. If the opposite is true, then pessimism and cynicism will be pervasive.

The emotional climate of the workplace is subtle yet powerful. If you've ever worked in a very negative atmosphere, you can testify to its impact. Sooner or later, most people find themselves behaving the same way. Psychologists explain this phenomenon with the term "social conformity," meaning that we receive subtle pressure to fit into a work environment. So if you are positive in a generally negative atmosphere, you'll find yourself feeling alone and out of place, because your fellow employees don't feel the same way. The pressure to become your coworkers is enormous. This being the case, it's a good idea to be sure that you share similar work attitudes with your coworkers. You want to be certain that they display attitudes and behaviors you want to emulate.

One way to begin creating a more positive atmosphere in your current work environment is to avoid the most negative people. Resist the temptation to engage in their games of "ain't it awful." No matter what the topic, these unfortunate individuals take a negative stance. Nothing is ever right. And they will always have something more awful to talk about than another person. We suggest two main ways of dealing with these toxic people: avoid them completely, or respond with only a neutral "Uh-huh." Either way, they will soon quit seeking you out as someone to talk to.

Seek out the positive people in your workplace. Find uplifting things to talk about. Learn to ask others questions that will draw out their best sides. For example, you can direct lunch conversation by asking about hobbies, favorite vacations, or other subjects that are fun to talk about. By doing so, you let others know that you want to focus on the positives, not the negatives.

When coworkers seek you out as someone to talk to about their problems, keep focused on helping that person to feel powerful in a difficult situation. After the individual has vented—remember, you're not a garbage can for someone to dump onto—you can begin to direct the conversation toward a solution to the issue. Saying things like, "I have every confidence that you can resolve this issue," or, "How can I help you resolve this dilemma?" will let the person know they've vented enough and the time has come to resolve the problem and get on with life. You have worked to rid yourself of negative messages about money so that your new positive beliefs can grow. Sometimes you have to work just as hard to stay positive in a workplace that is accustomed to negativity. The more you can model positive behaviors for your coworkers, the more likely you are to help in changing your work environment.

Sometimes, improving the atmosphere in your workplace is beyond your scope. Recognizing when this is the case is important to your mental health. In this situation you'll have to expend enough energy just keeping yourself positive, never mind trying to spread that attitude to others. In the meantime, polish your resume and begin talking to people who work in other companies. Do this informally at first, in ways that allow you to find out what the emotional climate is like. When you walk through another company, what do the employees look like? Are they generally smiling? Do they seem to have a lot of energy? Do they walk with a lively step, saying hello to each other in passing? These are signs of a positive workplace, one you might like to become a part of. This might seem like unusual research, but the rewards will be worth it. Once you find coworkers you can respect and enjoy, you will find yourself engaged in work that is satisfying and enjoyable.

## Finding a Job That Fits Your Money Values

One thing we all know for certain: The one constant in life is change. Change in one area of your life often leads you to changes in other areas as well. This dynamic will be true in both your workplace and personal life. In Chapter 14, we discuss the importance of holding a job that fits your new money messages and values. You may wish to reread that chapter as you assess the fit of your present job. Experiencing a clash between new values and those of the workplace is one of the first areas in which many people will notice discomfort. Your new messages may make it clear to you that you no longer belong in your current environment. This realization, as we have said, is one of the risks of change. Your new Self may need to find healthier job environments to play out the growth you have worked so hard to achieve. Change becomes difficult to maintain with the pressure of the old environment.

Family therapists have long been aware of the potential problems of change. They tell us that if one member of the family develops new, healthier ways of relating, then goes back into the same family system, friction is unavoidable. Families will frequently pressure the person exhibiting new behaviors to change back to continue to fit in. Has this phenomenon ever happened to you? This happens not because our families want us to be unhappy, but because they are likely to cling to that which is most familiar.

In a similar manner, as you begin to live out your revised money messages, your coworkers will either welcome the new you or lean on you to change back. The first scenario means that you are probably in the right place since coworkers who support your growth and change are to be cherished. All too often, however, the second scenario will be the one you have to face. If your new beliefs and the resulting statements about money are met with sarcasm or ridicule, you can be fairly certain that you will be making a change soon. The feeling of no longer fitting in will be your incentive to make some sort of adjustment, be it leaving for a new job or being less willing to participate in the negative aspects of your current work situation. As you learn to tune in to yourself, you will know what changes you need to make to enhance your work life. A woman in one of our workshops told of returning to her job as a part-time college faculty member after restructuring her beliefs about money.

> I found that I was no longer willing to attend the day long pre-semester faculty meeting. Once I realized that full-time faculty members were being paid to attend but those of us on part-time contracts were supposed to give our time away, I decided this no longer fit for me. I refuse to give my time away to an employer who doesn't value me in the same way as other faculty members. This didn't mean I was giving less to my students, it just meant I was beginning to weigh my values more carefully in my decision-making process. I was able to choose where I wanted to invest my precious time.

Another woman told of needing to find another job. "After redesigning my attitudes, I found that I didn't want to stay with my current position. I found the constant rumors about downsizing and layoffs were affecting my state of mind. My coworkers were becoming more anxious and fearful. I decided to look for a more positive atmosphere that was nurturing for me."

## Understanding Motivation

To accurately assess your work life, you need to understand what motivates you in your work. Does your motivation come from within yourself or from sources outside yourself? Intrinsic motivation, coming from within, leaves us in a much healthier position in the workplace. If the source of our motivation is internal, we find ourselves working for the satisfaction and positive feelings that come from a job well done, whether it is making a superior product, providing excellent service, or creatively managing the employees under our supervision. Financial rewards aren't ignored; they simply are put in their proper place. We feel a kinship with our fellow employees as we move with them toward a common goal. Intrinsically motivated employees are more able to make positive decisions because they can identify and focus on what is truly important. Further, they are more likely to be creative and produce a higher quality of work. Psychologists studying motivation in the workplace find that these are the employees who are most likely to thrive on challenge, complexity, and surprise in their work. Employees motivated by extrinsic rewards are more likely to see complexity and challenge as something to be avoided because these elements are seen as barriers to reaching the ultimate goal—money. Extrinsic rewards have a way of clouding our vision.

Being clear on our motivation for working means we are less likely to get caught in the trap of working for money alone, or, even more destructive, working to feel important. Both these attitudes are dangerous in a subtle way. They set us up to be workaholics, constantly striving for a goal we can never reach. Our work is important but it should not define who we are as individuals. Neither should money. Remember all the different aspects to your Inner Self? We need to have both work and money in their appropriate place to keep our vision clear and healthy. Thus, a merit raise for work well done becomes a tangible recognition of our work but not of our worth. Our healthy view of money and the resulting clarity of vision allow us to separate one from the other. We are not our work. Work does not determine our worth. We keep in mind the vision of our total Inner Self.

Another aspect of a clear vision in the workplace is self-knowledge. The woman with enough knowledge about herself is well equipped to make sound decisions regarding her future. She knows the value of her skills in the marketplace and is comfortable asking for what she deserves. This comfort is balanced by her knowledge that not everything is decided on the basis of money. Thus, she is free to decide her future not from a position of fear or pressure from others, but rather from a vision of how she wants her life to be. In a workshop, Pat told of her decision to not apply for a higher position within her place of employment:

> Moving up to that next step meant I would need to be available evenings and weekends if our organization was under pressure to get a report out. I knew I could do the work. I've even had people tell me I was wasted where I am. That's a lot of pressure, but I just don't want the added responsibility and stress. In my current job, I can be home with my family at night and right now, that's my priority. And I don't feel like I'm wasting away. I feel like I'm living the balanced life I want.

In a similar vein, Clarice shared her story.

> My boss asked me to apply for the unit supervisor's position and couldn't believe that I chose not to. I thought long and hard about making a change and realized that I'm happy where I am. I love being a secretary. I love the organization and the detail work involved in turning out accurate, professional level documents. The thought of needing to schedule everyone's work and tell people when they can have lunch and breaks seemed like something that would be really unpleasant. The extra money would have been nice but not nice enough to take a position that is so not me!

We applaud those women for their self-knowledge. Living your own vision is not always easy. But the rewards are worth it.

## Self-Esteem and Your Work Life

The concept of self-esteem has been thoroughly misunderstood and much maligned in the popular press. Too many articles about self-esteem promise an easy, feel-good fix. Such quick-fix proponents would lead us to believe we can raise our self-esteem by merely mouthing some positive saying about ourselves. Or that school teachers can give or withhold self-esteem by promoting or failing children regardless of what the children earn by their actions. Or that bosses can give us self-esteem by rewarding us with raises. A recent newspaper cartoon exemplified the extent of misunderstanding that abounds. In the cartoon, a small baby was driving the family car while the parents sat helpless in the back seat. The caption read, "There's such a thing as promoting too much self-esteem." With these types of misconceptions all too common, no wonder many of us are confused about self-esteem, and may even feel a little embarrassed discussing it. If we can't define it accurately, if we misunderstand what it really is, how can we hope to have positive self-esteem and have it work for us?

This confusion is likely to spill over into our work life. If we have bought into the mistaken idea that self-esteem can be given artificially from an external source, is it any wonder we aren't clear on how self-esteem fits with money?

True self-esteem is not something that comes from an outside source. In reality, self-esteem is an internal picture we carry of ourselves, derived from our self-evaluation in two main areas—competency and worthiness, two qualities that can only be earned. They can't be given. They certainly can't be purchased, no matter how much money one has. Thus, this accurate definition of self-esteem complements our new money messages, and our redesigned money messages work to help us develop true self-esteem.

Having our money messages straight and clear gives us yet another potential growth opportunity—that of letting our work enhance our self-esteem. Let's see how this happens.

With our new awareness of money as a tool, we are free of the old unhealthy ways of defining ourselves. We aren't working to define ourselves, we already have a healthy self-definition based on who we are internally. The work we do is a reflection—not the source—of our competence and worthiness. Thus, as we look at our work lives, we need to ask if this job reflects how we define ourselves. Are we doing what fits for us? Are we able to use our talents and skills in a way that complements who we are? Can we grow and develop or must we remain stagnant? Is this work an extension of our Inner Self? Working in a job that truly reflects who we are and allows us to grow builds self-esteem. Staying in a dead-end job with no opportunities will stifle self-esteem. If we are to use our work lives to enhance self-esteem, we need to be sure we are in the job that fits us.

Our work life can further build self-esteem by giving us appropriate opportunities to take risks. By engaging in risk-taking behavior, we know what we are capable of. Again, a career with no risk is safe, but it retards our growth in a soul-deadening way. As we face new challenges in our work, our self-esteem increases because of what we risk. Learning a new skill, succeeding in a training program, successfully supervising a difficult employee are all opportunities to build self-esteem. A worker with high self-esteem is willing to take risks. With each risk, regardless of the outcome, comes positive self-esteem because learning happens. With positive self-esteem comes the willingness to take new risks. The cycle is a satisfying one.

Self-esteem is also enhanced by the feeling that we are making a difference in an organization. As we influence, educate, guide, or direct others, we make a difference. When we produce or sell a product we can take pride in, we have an impact. If we believe in the mission of our organization, we set ourselves up to have high self-esteem. We know that women operate from a relational framework. That is, women focus on connections with others. We enjoy being cooperative and doing so adds to our self-esteem. Again, having a healthy relationship with money frees up energy for focusing on relationships and cooperation. We want to feel we make a difference in what we do. Having our money messages clear means we can find what is satisfying for us in our work.

Our work life can enhance or degrade our self-esteem. Our new clarity and comfort about our money messages give us a new freedom to seek out work opportunities that are growth producing and to help us move toward high self-esteem that is genuine and reality based.

Developing a positive relationship with money while ridding ourselves of the old, unhealthy messages, has implications for our lives beyond the immediate issue of money. Getting healthy in one aspect of our lives leads us to the desire to be healthy in other areas as well. Moving into a more positive relationship with our work and our work environment is a natural step to take in making the totality of our lives healthy.

# $\mathcal{T}$eaching Our Daughters About Money

As we become more and more at ease with finances and watch our new selves develop, we are ready for that important next step: helping the girls in our lives acquire healthy money messages. This new generation of young women can benefit from our struggles as they grow into better ways of coping with the world. Don't ever underestimate the impact you can have. One of our workshop participants told of a great aunt who had strongly impacted her life by being a nonconformist who rewrote family messages. As she told the story:

> Great Aunt Harriet was the eccentric in the family. Never married, she ran her own business, invested her own money, and traveled to exotic places, all without the help or permission of a man! I was aware she was regarded as odd by other family members, but there was also a sneaking sense of admiration in the voices of my mother and other female relatives when they talked about Aunt Harriet. Besides, it always seemed as if she was really enjoying life. Watching her example gave me the courage to forge my own path, to be independent, to be different.

We like to think that all women can be a Great Aunt Harriet, providing a positive role model for developing a healthy relationship with money. We can make a difference in the lives of our girls by challenging family messages, revising societal messages, and providing for positive planning.

## Challenging Family Messages

Just as our own family messages color our dealings with money, so the messages we send the girls in our lives will empower or depower them. We can transfer our fears or our courage, our capability or our inability. This being true, we need to look carefully at messages we give, weeding out those with any gender-based limitations. We want to be sure we are giving both our girls and our boys the "Yes, you can!" message. Both genders need equal opportunities for learning to deal with money in a healthy way. We can encourage both our daughters and sons to use money as a tool by helping them grow up with healthy expectations about wise spending, saving, investing, and charitable giving.

Both girls and boys need money of their own even at a young age so they will learn to be comfortable with it and to use it wisely. Some families give allowances, others teach about money through chores children perform for pay. Child psychologists debate about the wisdom of simply giving an allowance or tying that money to completing household chores. Regardless, choose the approach that makes sense to you. Discuss with your children ways to handle the money. Help them develop a balance between saving and spending. We generally recommend that children be encouraged to save half of the money they earn—gifts are in a different category. When your children are ready to open a savings account, take them to a financial institution so they can handle the transaction. Let them make their deposits. Avoid the temptation to do all this for them. Teach them how to read an account statement.

When discussing guidelines for money with your children, be

sure that a true discussion is going on. They must have input into the creation of the "family money guide"; otherwise, they won't participate. After they have saved half of their weekly allowance, they may want to do whatever they wish with the rest. Guiding children's choices is an important parental task. Dictating those choices is usually a mistake. Whether the rest of the money gets spent on a Saturday afternoon at an arcade or saved for a new bicycle or donated to charity, it's supporting the child's choice that is important. So is letting them know that support doesn't necessarily mean you agree with the decision.

Incidentally, if the money disappears at the arcade in one day, don't give in to any child-applied pressure for an advance on next week's allowance. One thing you're trying to teach is responsibility. That includes learning the difference between the unwise and the wise choices. Also resist any temptation to admonish your cashless child with "I told you so." This counterproductive statement can lead to a power struggle over who is "right." This is exactly the situation you're trying to avoid.

Regarding money gifts, we encourage parents to allow their children to use their own discretion about what to do with it. In addition to responsibility, you also want to nurture your children's confidence in their decision-making abilities. Hopefully they have as much enthusiasm about watching their money grow in savings, a money market, or other investment as they do about spending it.

You are helping create new money messages, developing positive habits about handling money, and demystifying the whole subject. By involving children in deciding what to do with their money, you are eliminating money as a potential focus for power struggles. Giving children the opportunity to learn about money is important. Grown-ups can give guidance about how much to spend, save, invest, and give away, but children need to have the funds with which to practice. Hands-on learning is always the most powerful way to turn mistakes into better ways of doing things.

We also need to give the same earning opportunities to our daughters that we give to our sons. If we give the boys business opportunities, we need to do the same for our girls. If our sons get money to invest, so should our daughters. If shares of stock or mutual funds are given as a holiday gift, they should be given to both boys and girls. As we encourage our sons to begin career planning early in life, we need to give our daughters the same messages. Courage and independence need not be limited by gender. This new way of thinking will call for constant attention to our own fears and biases. As we have learned, these early messages can be subtle yet strong. We will be continually revising our old messages in view of the new information our growing awareness gives us.

We need to be aware of our power as a role model in the lives of our girls. Our own feelings about money pack a powerful impact as we attempt to pass on healthy attitudes to young women. Anyone who has been around children is keenly aware that they do as we do, not as we say. In our relationships, we need to model equality, competence, and shared responsibility about handling money. We discuss finances openly with our partners, and resist the old game-playing, manipulative behaviors we may have seen modeled in our own families. There's nothing like working at setting a positive example to bring out our most positive behavior. Our girls can see healthy money relationships and decide that *this* is how life is supposed to be.

Further, we need to act honestly and courageously as we discuss money with the young women in our lives. Money outranks sex as a taboo topic in poll after poll; everything in our social training tells us it's *not* okay to talk about money. One woman we know struggled with her discomfort in talking to her niece about money issues, yet she didn't want her niece to live with the same negative family messages she had. She finally solved the problem by first discussing her discomfort with her niece. She was able to explain that her issues came from past messages, not current realities. Once her feelings were out in the open, talking about money messages was much easier. The aunt found her niece understanding and receptive to what she had to say. "I believe that dealing with my fears brought us closer," she reported. "My niece could understand the importance of my message, and it was one more chance for me to face some of my old money stuff."

Our growing comfort in dealing with the topic of money benefits the girls in our lives. We model making space in our lives for money in its most healthy aspect. Money loses its mystique and becomes a tool for fostering growth and well-being. We understand the ebb and flow of money just as we do the ebb and flow of our energy. We no longer need to struggle with our fears, and the young women in our lives are inspired and taught by our attitudes.

In looking at our past money messages, we need to credit the strengths we got from our families as well as acknowledge the limitations. The family can be a buffer against societal messages. Examples of the women in our lives who have broken with tradition to financially support their families can inspire us and help us rewrite the messages of society. For example, Diane never believed the societal promise that a prince would someday take care of her. The sudden deaths of two uncles, both in their twenties with wives and children, taught her that regardless of how good a picture looks, it can fade all too quickly. She was aware of the financial chaos that followed for the survivors and learned by the age of ten that she had better be able to support herself. The strong women in our families are the ones who help us see that we can take care of ourselves. This strength is an example we want to demonstrate for our daughters, nieces, and other important young women in our lives.

## Revising Societal Messages

Psychologist Mary Pipher chronicles the impact of what she terms our dysfunctional culture on the lives of our adolescent girls. Our society's overemphasis on money, sex, and violence wreaks the havoc she describes in her book *Reviving Ophelia: Saving the Selves of Adolescent Girls*. Helping our adolescent girls sort through these messages and rewrite them in a way that works is a formidable task. In the case of money messages, we can proceed in several ways. To begin with, we must help our girls place money in a proper perspective by helping them approach consumerism in a healthier way. This is no easy task. After all, we live in a society where the typical child views an average of 20,000 television ads in a year! To further compound the problem, some toy stores now provide children the opportunity to register for the gifts they want, much like brides have done for generations. This vision of children marching down toy aisles, electronically scanning their TV-prompted version of heart's desires into a computer, tells us how much work we have ahead. So, how do we proceed?

Knowing that young people have a built-in hypocrisy detector, we must have our own focus clear before we can hope to speak to them about cultivating a healthy relationship with money. Just as we can't urge our adolescents not to smoke if we ourselves are addicted, so we must have our own money priorities straight. For example, when we keep our focus on the role money can have in enhancing our life's work, we can talk honestly and without hypocrisy. Here are some actions we can take:

• We can help girls learn to distinguish between a need and a want. This is a critical part of breaking the hold of excess consumerism. Most of us would define a need as something we must have to survive, and a want as something we would like to have. Defining the concept is not a problem; however, putting the definition into action may take some strength. As adults, we are not immune to the pull of excess consumerism. We can help girls (and ourselves) do a brief economic analysis, as we ask: "Do I really need this item or do I merely want it? If I really want it, how much it is worth to me? Three hours of work time, four? How much use will I get out of it? Is it truly worth my money?" This kind of questioning helps us evaluate how strongly we desire an item and gives the choice back to the consumer, where it rightly belongs. Notice, also, that these questions are analytical, not judgmental. Helping our girls become conscious of their choices is excellent training for shopping and life.

• We can help girls develop a healthy self-esteem that is based on capability and accomplishment rather than on possessing this product or that item of clothing. We know from research that the self-esteem of girls takes a dramatic drop as they enter junior high school or middle school. They are going through many physical changes that are far more noticeable than what boys are experiencing. At the same time, adolescent society is designed to give boys a stage for their abilities, especially in sports, along with public acknowledgments of success. Girls have few such vehicles. We have even heard some adolescent females say they downplay their intelligence because so many boys are uncomfortable around smart girls. The groundwork is set for the diminishing of the young woman's self-esteem throughout her adolescence. The tragedy compounds itself because regaining self-esteem as a female adult is very difficult.

With this awareness, however, we can make a major effort to be there for them by providing support to help them weather the storms of adolescence. We also need to help them learn how to question cultural values that say you must look a certain way to matter. We can encourage our girls to look within themselves for strengths and abilities that don't depend on excessive consumption or unrealistic images. And we can help them acknowledge and celebrate their unique gifts.

• We can teach girls to see the difference between fantasy and reality. The vision of the prince still exists in our media and our lives, but we can help our daughters understand that this fits in the same category as the tooth fairy—a pleasant diversion when we are young, but not something to carry into adulthood.

## Providing for Positive Planning

If we are to teach our girls new ways of being toward the issue of money, we must also give them some concrete information and help them make some plans for their futures. As we stated earlier, hands-on knowledge is the surest way of imparting new ideas. Here are some suggestions for doing just that:

• We can give our girls the tools early on to make money knowledge (and comfort) an integral part of their lives. Helping young women start an investment club is an exciting and practical way to provide firsthand knowledge of how the stock market works. Introduce them to the concept, instruct them in how an investment club works, then get out of the way and let them run it. These groups are especially effective when the young women's mothers have their own investment club. The experience adds a whole new dimension to dinner-table discussions!

• We also want to encourage our girls to form the habit of saving regularly but with a new twist. Encourage them to research the rates of various saving options to help them find the best place to keep their savings. Teach them to read the financial pages of the daily newspaper. With our help, girls can make decisions about money and practice those skills they will need as adults. Again, the message we want to provide is that money is a tool that, when managed skillfully, can help us fulfill our life's purpose. As adults we have struggled with our money issues. How much easier life would be to grow into comfort about the topic of money and not have to undo fears as we did.

• We can give money with the stipulation that it is to be invested to help our daughters get started on the road to financial awareness. We know a woman whose parents gave her a chunk of money at age twelve, introduced her to the family's financial planner, and started her on her way toward a healthy relationship with money.

This was her money to invest as she saw fit. She was encouraged, but not required, to seek parental advice. And her parents had the wisdom to avoid offering advice when it wasn't sought. Regardless of the size of the seed money, watching their own money grow as a direct result of their efforts can help girls feel powerful around the issue of money.

• We can give our girls information about money. Books are always a great gift. Some of them are written with young people in mind and deal with money management and investing. One such book written specifically for girls has the wonderful title *No More Frogs to Kiss: 99 Ways to Give Economic Power to Girls*.[1] As we encourage girls to take an interest in finance and economics, we broaden their range of choices and increase their personal power and confidence.

• We can keep our girls conscious of the career options open to them and foster the expectation of success. Again, knowing the research on girls' self-esteem, we need to be especially vigilant around the time of junior high to keep girls from becoming discouraged about their futures. There are several ways to do this. For example, Bonnie tells of her parents establishing a college fund for her, before she even knew what college was. "I heard my parents talk about the college fund and how important it was. It took awhile before I really understood what it was all about. But, because of my knowledge of this fund, I grew up with the expectation that I would go to college. It was never a question of whether I'd go to school, only where and when." We may also want to engage our daughters in making decisions about how a college fund is to be invested. This, of course, requires becoming educated about different types of investment instruments, their purpose, and risk factors.

• Along with encouraging education beyond high school, we need to make certain young women learn about computers, the tool of the new millennium. Our daughters need skills and comfort with computers to cope with the information age. As a painless introduction, we might help them track their investments on the Internet or manage their finances with a money management program. Along with computers go math and science courses so that their career choices are not limited. After all, we know that by taking only basic math and ignoring anything beyond, 66 percent of possible careers are eliminated.

• Participating in the Take Our Daughters to Work movement is a great way to foster awareness of career possibilities. We need to be conscious of the potential impact this practice can have. Further, we suggest not limiting ourselves to one day each year to introduce our daughters to the workplace. The more often they can visit the better. As we take pride in our careers and make them a fulfilling part of our lives, we can demonstrate this to our daughters. Our work is no longer something to be discounted or seen merely as a diversion while we wait for Mr. Right to arrive. They can see the reality of exchanging skills for money and the satisfaction that can come from having a healthy relationship with both work and money.

As we abandon the old fear-based messages about money, we allow our daughters to do so as well. Our attitudes toward money issues will demonstrate that being in charge of our own lives is the way to live. Do we want our daughters to grow up fearful and dependent or strong and independent? The answer to that is clear. As we rid ourselves of unhealthy money messages, replacing them with positive, empowering beliefs, we teach the girls in our lives to do the same. We serve as role models to the new generation—an awesome responsibility and an exciting challenge.

*Chapter Seventeen*

# Decisions, Decisions, or What Do I Do Now?

Increased awareness brings both discomfort and promise. Discomfort comes from the recognition that it's time to make some changes as well as from the knowledge that change, by its very nature, is bound to be unsettling. Promise arises from adopting healthier, more productive attitudes. As you worked your way through this book, focusing on your old messages and seeing how they play out in current behaviors, you may have identified changes you wish to make in your life right now. These changes require you to make some new decisions as you discard the attitudes and behaviors that no longer work and add others that will be more beneficial. Let's look at some of the decisions ahead.

## Decision One: What Is My Ideal Relationship to Money?

As we noted in Chapter 11, we receive a wide range of responses when we ask women to describe their ideal relationship with money. Some women are content to have a little more than their needs. One woman modestly wished that, "I would always have an extra $100 more than I need." An educator wanted "to have more than my needs, but a little less than all my wants."

Other women wished for wealth as they defined an ideal relationship to money. "Fabulously wealthy," said Shirley, a business owner. She continued, "To give anonymously to those I wish and make a significant financial contribution to causes I believe in." Anita, a scientist, replied that she wanted "to earn a lot and to understand how to earn more."

On yet another point on the continuum were the women who wished to have money play a very minor role in their lives. A student wanted to do away with money altogether, as she noted that her ideal relationship was "not to have to have it. I like the barter system." A vocational counselor stated that her ideal relationship "is not to have a relationship with money." An editor told us, "I think it would just be there. I wouldn't have to think about it."

This wide range of responses points out our confusion over the appropriate place money should occupy in our lives. What comments did you make initially concerning your ideal relationship to money? The way you responded reflects your personal challenges with finding the balance for money in your own life.

Taking into account what you now know about your own attitudes and perceptions regarding money, what changes do you wish to make in your definition of an ideal relationship to money? Write your new response here:

My ideal relationship with money is _____

_____.

## Decision Two: Where Does Money Fit Into My Career Goals?

Women must affirm continuously their right to be in a career that pays a salary reflective of their skills and abilities. Both authors have worked in career counseling and have found that often women have difficulty including salary expectations as part of their career plans. That conditioned response of not talking about money because women are not supposed to kicks in. The response can be powerful; it can also be limiting! Kay recalls teaching a career class in which an informational interview was part of the course requirements. The students were to go out into the community and interview a person in a career they were considering. The women in the group seemed to freeze when it came to asking about salary potential, expressing great reluctance to do so. "I can't ask about money. It's just not right," responded one female student.

The more we begin to acknowledge the importance of money in our lives, the easier it is to ask for what we deserve and to see money as having a place in our career plans. Again, we are not suggesting that women make money the ultimate measure of the fitness of a career plan. We *are* encouraging women to see it as part of the bigger picture and not ignore it as we have in the past. Keeping money issues in balance requires that we have a goal in mind. It's OK to want a reasonable salary for our work and to desire a comfortable lifestyle. If we are to be in control of our lives, these decisions play a critical role.

A further piece of the puzzle is the need to keep our volunteer work in perspective. As discussed in Chapter 9, we no longer have to give our talents away unless we clearly choose to. As we develop a more powerful relationship with money, this perspective becomes easier to achieve. We know the difference between what we deserve for our work and what we freely give because it makes the world a better place. Making this distinction helps us. Such a decision requires conscious thought. That is the message we hope to deliver to the women reading this book: By keeping money in our consciousness, we free ourselves to let it go. A curious paradox, isn't it?

## Decision Three: Who Handles My Money?

There is no longer any doubt that we need to pay attention to our financial affairs. We know that waiting for the prince or blindly turning responsibility over to someone else is doomed to failure. Taking care of our own finances does not have to be an onerous chore, however, and we do have choices in how we will discharge this responsibility. As Catherine, a research specialist, summed it up, "Do it yourself or pay someone to do it for you." Some women prefer to do all the financial work themselves, from managing the day-to-day checking account to handling their own investments. If this is your choice and you are comfortable doing so, more power to you. We salute your skill and courage.

Others of us want to have a knowledge of our affairs but have someone else handle the details. This is also a valid choice. Again, the whole point of this book centers on *taking responsibility for the choices we make.* Find a financial manager with whom you can feel comfortable. The manager should be someone who treats you with respect, answers all your questions, goes over a point as many times as you need in order to understand it, and never, ever, implies you are stupid for not knowing what she knows.

## Decision Four: How Do I Deal With Money If I Am in a Relationship?

Being in a relationship does not free us from needing to know where our money is going. We still have a responsibility. By now, we are well aware of this reality. Being in a relationship does require that we give additional thought to how we will handle finances as part of a couple. Joint or separate checking accounts? Do we join our savings or not? What about property purchases? What about estate planning?

We need to be clear about our own issues so that we can translate them into couplehood. Then we need to discuss money issues clearly with our partner to ensure that we are keeping our financial balance in a way that fits who we are.

This is another tough task women face as we move to acknowledge our power where money is concerned. Know if you need help in this area. You may need to discuss this with an attorney, a financial planner, or both. It is beyond the scope of this book to tell you how to handle this thorny issue. Our task is to encourage you to include it in your plan as you take control of your financial life.

## Decision Five: In What Other Ways Can I Take Charge of My Financial Life?

Some women have found that forming support groups on the issue of money enables them to maintain their balance. They find encouragement from others for facing up to their fears and foibles, and report that they are growing in confidence and capability. You may know a group of compatible women who would be interested in forming such a group.

A second possibility is an investment club. Marge, the director of a woman's retreat center, described how being in this type of group has affected her. "I have always 'spaced out' about this kind of stuff and am trying to get at least a minimal grip on it—to be a big girl— and the all-female energy and support help a lot. It's OK to ask dumb questions and admit confusion!"

Women in increasing numbers are finding that investment clubs are a great way to learn about the stock market. You may have heard of the Beardstown Ladies, an investment club that parlayed its knowledge into success in the stock market as well as into a best-selling book. Many women's groups are sponsoring investment clubs. Your public library or nearest bookstore has information on how to form an investment club, so if this is your choice, you will find plenty of advice for getting started. You can gather a group of like-minded women and learn to invest together.

Groups can be a wonderful way to learn new skills and develop knowledge in any field. They are particularly effective when it comes to learning about the somewhat scary area of finance and investing because of the support they provide. Nancy, a self-employed psychotherapist, started out learning about investing by joining an investment club. The club gave her the knowledge and confidence to go it on her own, and she currently handles all her own investments as a means of retirement planning. "When I think about where I started and where I am now, it is amazing," she said in describing her growth. She continued, "Handling my own investments gives me a sense of control over my destiny I never thought I could have." Now *that's* power!

The decisions facing us as we change our money attitudes can seem overwhelming. There is much to learn and do. Money *is* a challenging issue for women and we commend your courage in looking at how it plays out in your life. We hope that you have taken your curiosity along on this trek and that you are always intrigued about how to make your relationship with money serve you in positive ways. By now you have an understanding of the issues that resonate for you and have identified changes you wish to make. You will continue to redefine your issues and make changes as you move toward your ideal relationship with money.

Susan reflected this redefining process when she wrote, "My ideal is to be able to challenge my belief system/perception to the point of not having money be such a primary focus of my thinking, to take back my power by more successfully managing my money, separating my individual worth from 'amounts' of money earned or given."

Looking at our lives and changing our money attitudes to reclaim the feminine power of money is sometimes frustrating and painful. It is also an exciting, challenging, and growth-filled journey. Happy traveling!

*Epilogue*

# The Maiden and the Marketplace Revisited

Not so long ago and just down the block lived a young woman. This woman wanted to have a career that would challenge her creativity and provide her with a solid income. So she listened carefully to the teachings of her college instructors. Sometimes she would hear her coworkers at her part-time job discussing retirement packages and 401(k)s. She knew exactly what they were talking about.

She lived with her mother and grandmother and would also listen to their wisdom. Her grandmother was fond of looking at the young woman and saying, "You're the one who is going to make a lot of money." She liked to hear these words from her grandmother because they were said with such warmth and reassurance. Besides, she had been hearing them since she was a child.

Her mother also gave her wise words about money. "Some day your prince may come," she liked to say, "but you need to have your own career and money even when he does." Then she would remind the young woman that her own father, rest his soul, was a loving provider. No one expected him to depart this Earth at so young an age. The young woman knew very well the challenges her mother had in being the sole support of the family.

One day, her grandmother gave the young woman $1,000 to invest in the stock market. "See what you can do with it," she said encouragingly. So the woman began to research investments. She subscribed to magazines that dealt with investing. She talked with stock brokers. They encouraged her to invest with them. They told her how safe her money would be with them and even advised her against some investments they said would be too risky. But she knew these stocks were expected to grow. She watched the financial programs on cable TV and talked with other women who were interested in investing.

Then she heard about groups of wise women called investment clubs. These groups sounded good to the young woman. So she gathered several of her friends and her mother and grandmother, and they pooled their money, forming their own investment club. With the support of the group, they became very astute investors.

As the years passed, their money grew so much that several women quit their jobs and pursued what they truly loved to do. One woman devoted herself to fund-raising for her favorite charity. Another mentored women entrepreneurs. Several others joined forces to push for legislative changes requiring that every high school student in the state take a course in money management. They also worked out the curriculum.

The young woman, her mother, and grandmother opened their own financial consulting business, empowering other women to have positive relationships with money. At last report they were considering franchising throughout the country.

Their book will be out in the spring.

# References

## Chapter Two: Exploring Your Money Messages

1. Olivia Mellan, *Money Harmony* (New York: Walker and Company, 1994), p. 120.
2. Ibid., p. 121.
3. Ibid., p. 122.
4. Ibid., p. 123.
5. James Doyle and Michele Paludi, *Sex and Gender: The Human Experience* (Madison, WI: Brown & Benchmark, 1995), p. 103.
6. Monica McGoldrick, *You Can Go Home Again: Reconnecting With Your Family* (New York: W.W. Norton & Company, 1995), p. 273.

## Chapter Three: Those Sneaky Fairy Tales

1. Mark Nelson and Dale Dauten, "De-link Salary From Job Before Negotiating With an Employer," *The Arizona Daily Star*, Nov. 25, 1996, p. 6D.

## Chapter Four: Taking Your Power Back

1. Amy Gage, "Women & Money: A Wake Up Call," *The Arizona Daily Star*, Sept. 26, 1994, pp. 8–9D.
2. Ibid., p. 8.

3. Kathy Kristof, "Women Being Wooed as Rising Financial Force," *The Arizona Daily Star*, June 10, 1996, p. 2D.

4. Ann Landi, "Marriage and Money: Some Unromantic Advice," *New Woman*, Feb. 1996, pp. 102–105.

5. Gage, "Women & Money," p. 8.

6. Bloomberg Business News, "Women More Savvy Investors," *The Arizona Daily Star*, January 17, 1998, p. 1C.

7. James Doyle and Michele Paludi, *Sex and Gender: The Human Experience* (Madison, WI: Brown & Benchmark, 1995), p.103.

8. Peggy Orenstein, *Schoolgirls: Young Women, Self-Esteem and the Confidence Gap* (New York: Doubleday, 1994).

9. Bonnie Golden and Kay Lesh, *Building Self-Esteem: Strategies for Success in School—and Beyond* (Scottsdale, AZ: Gorsuch Scarisbrick, 1994).

## Chapter Six: The Treadmill to Nowhere

1. Harriet Goldhor Lerner, *The Dance of Anger: A Woman's Guide To Changing Patterns of Intimate Relationships* (New York: Harper & Row, 1985).

## Chapter Seven: Burying Your Head in the Coins

1. Gannet News Service, "Double Standard Makes Women Feel Guilty About Earning Money," *Tucson Citizen*, First Edition, Nov. 19, 1993.

2. Mary Deibel, "Fewer Than 1 in 5 Are Knowledgeable Investors," *The Arizona Daily Star*, May 15, 1996, p. 4B.

3. Ibid., p. 4B.

4. Bloomberg Business News, "Women More Savvy Investors," *The Arizona Daily Star*, January 17, 1998, p. 1C.

5. Betty Lehan Harragan, *Games Your Mother Never Taught You* (New York: Warner Books, 1977).

6. Penelope Wang, "How Brokers Mistreat Women," *Money*, June 1994, p. 108.

7. Ibid., p. 110.

8. "You and Your Money—A Financial Handbook for Women," Merrill, Lynch, Pierce, Fenner & Smith, Inc., 1996, p. 3.

9. Anne Willette, "Women Face Shaky Retirement," *Tucson Citizen*, May 29, 1996, p. 4B.

10. Kathy Kristof, "Women Being Wooed as Rising Financial Force," *The Arizona Daily Star*, June 10, 1996, p. 2D.

11. Willette, "Women Face Shaky Retirement."

12. Amy Gage, "Women & Money: A Wake Up Call," *The Arizona Daily Star*, Sept. 26, 1994, pp. 8–9D.

13. Betsy Carter, "Moment Mania," *New Woman*, Oct., 1995, p. 49.

14. Carin Rubenstein, "New Woman's Report on Self-Esteem," *New Woman*, Oct., 1992, p. 60.

15. Jean Bodnar, "What Women Can Teach Men About Money: Women Have Different, and Sometimes Better, Attitudes Than Men," *Kiplinger's Personal Finance Magazine*, July 1994, p. 87.

16. John Hendren, "Finances Worry Women More," *Tucson Citizen*, May 9, 1996, p. 8C.

17. Bodnar, "What Women Can Teach," p. 88.

18. Ibid.

19. Ibid., p. 87.

20. Gail Sheehy, "Why Women Fear They Will End Up Living in a Box Outside Bergdorf's," *Money*, Nov., 1996, p. 176.

21. "You and Your Money—A Financial Handbook for Women," Merrill, Lynch, Pierce, Fenner & Smith, Inc., 1996, p. 3.

## Chapter Nine: To Give It Away or Not to Give It Away

1. Los Angeles Times–Washington Post News Service, "Poll: Women Business Owners Volunteer More," *Tucson Citizen*, June 4, 1996, p. 3C.

2. C Diane Ealy, *The Woman's Book of Creativity* (Hillsboro, OR: Beyond Words Publishing, 1995), pp. 49–51.

## Chapter Fifteen: Working for More Than Money

1. Dale Dauten, "Run, Do Not Walk, Away From a Soul-Killing Employer," *The Arizona Daily Star*, Jan. 28, 1998, p. 4B.
2. Paul D. Tieger and Barbara Barron-Tieger, *Do What You Are*, 2d edition (Boston, MA: Little, Brown and Company, 1995).

## Chapter Sixteen: Teaching Our Daughters About Money

1. Joline Godfrey, *No More Frogs to Kiss: 99 Ways to Give Economic Power to Girls* (New York: HarperCollins, 1995).

# *Index*